Multidimensional MINISTRY
FOR TODAY'S BLACK FAMILY

W9-CCS-812

9/07
CH

Multidimensional
MINISTRY
FOR TODAY'S BLACK FAMILY

JOHNNY B. HILL, PhD

FOREWORD BY WALLACE CHARLES SMITH

JUDSON PRESS
PUBLISHERS SINCE 1824
VALLEY FORGE, PA

MULTIDIMENSIONAL MINISTRY FOR TODAY'S BLACK FAMILY

Judson Press and the authors have made every effort to trace the ownership of all quotes. In the event of a question arising from the use of a quote, we regret any error made and will be pleased to make the necessary correction in future printings and editions of this book.

Bible quotations in this volume are from:
The New Revised Standard Version of the Bible (NRSV), copyright © 1989 by the Division of Christian Education of the National Council of the Churches of Christ in the United States of America. Used by permission. All rights reserved. HOLY BIBLE: *New International Version* (NIV), copyright © 1973, 1978, 1984. Used by permission of Zondervan. The New King James Version. Copyright © 1982 by Thomas Nelson, Inc. Used by permission. All rights reserved.

Library of Congress Cataloging-in-Publication Data

Multidimensional ministry for today's Black family / [edited by] Johnny B. Hill.
p. cm.
Includes bibliographical references.
ISBN 978-0-8170-1518-3 (pbk. : alk. paper) 1. African Americans—Religion.
2. Family—Religious aspects—Christianity. I. Hill, Johnny B.
BR563.N4M85 2007
259'.108996073—dc22

2007002964

Printed on recycled paper in the U.S.A.
First Edition, 2007.

To the beauty, strength,
and resilience of the black family.

CONTENTS

Foreword   xii
Wallace Charles Smith, DMin

Acknowledgments   ix

Introduction   xiv

1 / Grounded in Faith: The Church and   1
Black Family Life
Johnny B. Hill, PhD

2 / Elephants in the Pews: Confronting Silent   14
Issues in the Church
Sherrill McMillan, MD

3 / Gettin' Ready to Jump da Broom and   27
How to Make Your Good Thing Better!
Lorraine C. Blackman, PhD, LCSW, CFLE

4 / Exploring the Meaning and Possibilities   41
of Black Fatherhood Today
Edward P. Wimberly, PhD, Rueben Warren, DDS,
Anne Streaty Wimberly, PhD

5 / Black Men, the Church, and Family   57
in Hip-Hop Culture
Johnny B. Hill, PhD

6 / Yield Not to Temptation: Confronting   **69**
the Financial Challenges of the Black Family
Michael L. Cook, MDiv

7 / Models for Ministry to Black Families   **78**
Johnny B. Hill, PhD

8 / Practical Steps for Ministry to Black   **88**
Families in Today's World
Elizabeth Johnson Walker, PhD

9 / Revisiting the Church in the Life of   **100**
the Black Family: Then and Now
Wallace Charles Smith, DMin

Bibliography   **112**

About the Contributors   **121**

FOREWORD

In a political climate of faith-based philosophies and bootstrap initiatives, the black community in America remains mired in a world of poverty, inadequate educational systems, insufficient health care, and violence. The black church, historically, has been the force that steered black America through the realities of Jim Crow segregation, economic disadvantage, and institutionalized racism. During the 1990s and the first few years of the twenty-first century, a concerted effort was made to declare racism as ended and the ills of the black community as a product of its own making—in other words, blaming the victim for the victimization.

The advent of televangelism and the megachurch phenomenon added to a rising tide within the black church of those who acquiesced to conservative arguments. Many of these neo-black evangelicals seem to believe the church should not be involved in politics (although the moral majority has had no problem involving itself in politics as long as is conservative and Republican). While the church permitted itself the luxury of believing America had desisted from its retrenched de facto racism, warning lights began flashing that this was far from the case. While retreating from a so-called activist stance, the Supreme Court indicated by its rulings that it had actually become actively supportive of right-wing causes. Gaps in wages and income between blacks and whites, which had previously been closing, began to widen again. Test scores and overall academic performance for white, black, and Hispanic communities showed growing disparities.

Violent crime statistics soared upward. Drug proliferation in inner cities went unchallenged. HIV/AIDS infection among the urban poor were statistically identical to those in impoverished nations. Incarceration rates for blacks continued to rise as higher percentages of young black men were arrested under "three strikes and you're out" laws, thereby incurring longer and harsher jail sentences.

All of these facts mean the church needs to reexamine its present position and restore itself to the place of being the voice in black America for freedom and justice. It is not sufficient to have a fiery, exciting worship service if the community outside the church's walls is plagued by prostitution, drug deals, and gang wars. Many in the African American community feel it is time to break the silence.

It is unconscionable that more than 47 million Americans are without health care in the richest country in the history of the planet. In 2006 alone, 4.3 million new HIV/AIDS infections were reported, and 2.9 million people around the world died from AIDS, while pharmaceutical companies made record profits and refused to offer retroviral drugs at reasonable prices.[1]

There is no excuse for the rampant violence that has turned the streets of many American cities into shooting galleries, while police seem more intent on stopping people on highways for the crime of DWB—"driving while black."

During the days of slavery, the black church was the underground institution that stood in the gap. From the ranks of the black church emerged preachers who voiced a vision of liberation, lawyers who argued the case for freedom, and educators who prepared succeeding generations to shoulder the mantle of justice.

In the book of Esther, Mordecai encouraged Queen Esther, who was a Jew, not to keep silent while her people were under the threat of death from the Persian Empire. Mordecai suggested that Esther had been brought into the royal household for such a time as this. In much the same way, the black church today cannot keep silent. Our people live under the threat of death from poverty, violence, disease, and injustice. God has brought us to the world for such a time as this.

—Dr. Wallace Charles Smith
Author, *The Church in the Life of the Black Family*
President, Palmer Theological Seminary
Wynnewood, PA
Pastor, Shiloh Baptist Church
Washington, DC

NOTE

1. "Income, Poverty, and Health Insurance Coverage in the United States: 2005" (US Census Bureau, 2005); "World Health Organization (WHO) AIDS Epidemic Update" (December 2006).

ACKNOWLEDGMENTS

Many contributed to the development of this project. Initially it started as a conversation I had with Brenda Girton-Mitchell, of the National Council of Churches, and Arlene Tyler, president of the Women's Department of the Progressive National Baptist Church. These gifted women of God are to be commended for their vision and leadership in the inaugural Breaking the Silence for the Good of All People Conference and in helping to make this project a reality. The conference was held in August 2006 in Cincinnati, around the subject of how churches and the wider African American community can begin to "break the silence" and initiate an honest dialogue about the problems, as well as possible solutions, concerning African American families. Scholars, clergy, activists, and therapists gathered to discuss much of the subject matter of this book. They are to be thanked profusely for generating the ideas, strategies, and resources for ministry to families. Without their support of the conference and project, this book would not exist.

Much thanks is due Dr. Wallace Charles Smith who, more than a decade ago, brought the issue of family ministry to the forefront in his book *The Church in the Life of the Black Family*. (Judson Press, 1985). As president of Palmer Theological Seminary outside of Philadelphia and pastor of Shiloh Baptist Church in Washington DC, Dr. Smith continues to bridge the gap between the church and academy in meaningful and creative ways. This project would not be possible without his vision and persistent leadership.

I am also deeply thankful for the contributors who, despite their busy schedules, took time to be a part of this project. Each of them is an expert in his or her own field, and each has years of experience serving African American families. I thank them for their commitment to this project and for their dedicated service to the church and African American community at large.

I would certainly like to express my appreciation to Judson Press for their generous support of this project and the cause it represents. I am especially grateful to Linda Peavy and Rebecca Irwin-Diehl for their assistance throughout the process.

Finally, I celebrate and adore my wife, Trinia, whose love and ongoing devotion are unparalleled. I am constantly amazed by her grace and wisdom, which continue to be budding sources of inspiration for projects such as this. I also appreciate the support of my children, Jonathan and Regan, who, though small, are big in heart and spirit. Thank you.

INTRODUCTION

For decades the black family has thrived and overcome incredible odds, ranging from poverty, racism, and sexism to a host of other challenges. I am convinced that the resilience of the black family is, to a large extent, due to the power and vibrancy of the black church. We are a family-oriented people. We love family. We live family. The language of "brother" and "sister" saturates our church culture, which recognizes that faith in Jesus Christ brings individuals with no biological connection into a harmonious family relationship. That is not to say that the black church has not had its problems. We have all heard horror stories of church conflicts, scandals, payoffs, and ministerial misgivings. However, many churches and individuals are working on the front lines to provide faithful witness to black families across the nation in urban and rural settings. Small churches and big churches, country churches and city churches all share a common commitment to worship the Lord Jesus Christ and to make that worship meaningful in the lives of others.

In the times in which we live, the church and faithful believers have a real opportunity to "break the silence" surrounding the challenges facing today's black families—by beginning a serious debate on what is being done and what can be done to strengthen black families. Without question there is much to address. The sense of family within the church is not limited to the walls of the church. As Christians we are given a divine mandate to take our faith beyond the church to others. It has often been the case in black churches that we have been intentional about dealing with the social, political, and economic dynamics of the church's membership. Building on this rich heritage of addressing the whole person—mind, body, and spirit—is what holds the key to the church's capacity to turn the tide of challenging issues affecting the black family today.

We must think about the diverse needs of black families, including their material, spiritual, emotional, and psychological needs. We must engage in holistic ministry that addresses these multidimensional needs. And we must appeal to those who wish to reflect critically on the issues facing the black family, while also being accessible to practitioners and congregants who wish to establish or strengthen programs in their own churches.

The purpose of this project is twofold. First, we purpose to inform readers of the dynamics at work in the black family today. Because not all black families are the same, this requires dealing with the complexities of black family life, particularly within the urban context and as it relates to young parenting, the black middle class, and so on. If churches, leaders, and practitioners are not fully informed about the forces confronting black families, they will feel ill equipped to minister in meaningful and transformative ways.

Second, we intend to give practical strategies and models on ministry to black families. In addition to providing real-life case studies, we will delineate a detailed list and description of programs, organizations, offices, and individuals with whom churches can partner. Programs such as the Healthy Family Initiatives and the African American Healthy Marriage Initiative, Smart Marriages, National Institute for Responsible Fatherhood and Family Revitalization, and the National Fatherhood Initiative are some of the resources that will be highlighted.

More than anything, the purpose of this book is to inspire and equip believers for ministry to black families in today's world. Of course there are many more resources available than what can be included in these pages. We simply hope to create the space for conversation and mutual sharing in churches and among individuals about the crisis in the lives of black families everywhere.

The terms *African American* and *black* are used interchangeably throughout the study because the contributors bring a wealth of diverse perspectives to the topic. Experts in their fields, these contributors bring together years of professional experience, faith in Jesus Christ, and a determination to tackle the problems facing our families.

Chapter 1: Grounded in Faith: The Church and Black Family Life

This chapter establishes the basis for ministry to families as rooted in Scripture. It also reflects on how, historically, the church has played a fundamental role in supporting and sustaining black family life. Because the church is a faith community, ministry to family must be firmly rooted in Scripture and Christian theology. Here, readers will be guided through what it means for the church, as the broken and risen body of Jesus Christ, to engage in the ministry of healing, nurturing, and transforming black families in today's context. The contributor, Johnny B. Hill, suggests that ministry to black families must attend to three important areas: partnerships, education, and long-term follow-up. He looks at the historical importance of the church in the life of the black family and points out how the concept of "family," as a paradigm, can play a powerful role in building community and strengthening nuclear families.

Chapter 2: Elephants in the Pews: Confronting Silent Issues in the Church

In this chapter special attention is given to the psychological issues that confront black families. It also reflects on many of the reasons churches often remain silent on issues that can be associated with problems in the life of church leadership. Healing becomes the central theme as the chapter draws from the biblical paradigm of the "family of God." Author Sherrill McMillan, a minister and psychologist based at the Metropolitan Baptist Church in Washington, DC, takes on a number of pressing physical and mental health issues in the black church and offers practical solutions and remedies. Some of the themes discussed are marriage and family conflicts, sexual addictions, domestic violence, unhealthy behaviors, as well as spiritual, emotional, and psychological healing.

Chapter 3: Gettin' Ready to Jump da Broom and How to Make Your Good Thing Better!

Lorraine Blackman, professor in the School of Social Work at Indiana University, addresses the challenges of black families by focusing on the importance of strengthening black married life. Pointing out that only about one-third of all black households are led by two parents, she observes that the black church has a unique role in nurturing and sustaining black marriages and subsequently strengthening overall black family life. Dr. Blackman demonstrates that not only do couples thrive when they share a healthy, loving relationship, but they live longer, fare better financially, and increase the chance of raising well-balanced children. She also exposes some of the contradictions and challenges to celebrating marriage in churches, while offering viable solutions for overcoming these barriers.

Chapter 4: Exploring the Meaning and Possibilities of Black Fatherhood Today

Anne and Edward Wimberly and Rueben Warren take on the often neglected subject of black fatherhood in this chapter. As therapist theologian and medical professional respectively, these contributors trace the origins, development, and dynamics of black fatherhood, which they see as a product of complex social realities and childhood experiences. The authors thoroughly examine the root causes of "absentee fatherhood" and provide a compelling model for strengthening fatherhood and, subsequently, black family life. They believe that when churches are intentional about ministering to the needs of black fathers, those churches are paving the way for stronger and healthier families. Discussing the need for more intervention with the criminal justice system, advocacy, and therapy, the authors provide an exciting and dynamic approach to fatherhood and the black family.

Chapter 5: Black Men, the Church, and Family in Hip-Hop Culture

Particular social problems disproportionately impact African American males in their quest to perform the duties of family and fatherhood. In this chapter, Johnny B. Hill offers a critical appraisal of the spiritual and social forces at work in the life of black men and how those forces affect the entire family. The chapter also provides helpful solutions to strengthening and supporting black fathers. Hill gives critical thought to defining black fatherhood in today's culture as well as consideration of the serious impact of technology, incarceration, unemployment, and commercialism. The chapter concludes with a discussion of solutions and opportunities for reshaping the meaning of fatherhood.

Chapter 6: Yield Not to Temptation: Confronting the Financial Challenges of the Black Family

Because finances continue to be a major problem in black family life, Michael Cook offers practical resources for churches and individuals in their efforts to enhance the economic conditions of black families. Cook believes that faith in Jesus Christ and solid financial practices contribute to a healthy and thriving home life; therefore, he encourages families to take an honest assessment of their financial state of affairs and to identify the underlying reasons for profligate spending habits, Cook relates his own experience, tracing his childhood in a single-parent home in the projects of southeastern Georgia to his current career as a banker and consultant. He also provides meaningful tips to achieve a healthy financial lifestyle.

Chapter 7: Models for Ministry to Black Families

It is important to know exactly what a faithful and thriving family ministry looks like. So this chapter is devoted to reviewing outstanding programs from various churches. Churches considered as models vary in location (urban/suburban), size, and general resources available. In this chapter, author Johnny B. Hill explores the strengths and weaknesses of various models of ministry to black families, including churches, nonprofits, and advocacy groups. As this chapter reveals, there are exciting efforts taking place in communities around the country, which often go unnoticed. Churches, lay leaders, and individuals can find encouragement knowing they are not alone in their efforts to uplift the black family.

Chapter 8: Practical Steps for Ministry to Black Families in Today's World

In this chapter Elizabeth Johnson Walker, longtime marriage and family therapist in Atlanta, Georgia, presents some challenging and inspiring insights for individuals who wish to work with black families in today's world. Drawing from more than twenty years of experience, Walker claims that churches must recover the strengths of spirituality, community, and education as strategies for ministry to black families. Families look to the church for guidance, counseling, information, and overall support, she says, and congregations must be prepared to respond. This chapter also raises some critical and probing questions for churches, individuals, and organizations, encouraging them to make careful assessments of where they are and where they want to go.

Chapter 9: Revisiting the Church in the Life of the Black Family: Then and Now

In this final chapter, pastor and seminary professor Wallace Charles Smith returns to the subject of his classic book, *The Church in the Life of the Black Family.*[1] More than twenty years have passed since the publication of that volume, and Dr. Smith considers what has changed—and how things have stayed the same. He remains convinced that the church is the vehicle through which the needs of the black family may be met and transformed—not only through preaching and individual salvation but through service in the community and action in the public sphere.

It is with a great deal of enthusiasm and excitement that I invite you to read this volume—and to do so with a renewed sense of hope in celebrating the church and black family. I encourage you to take full advantage of the resources, insights, recommendations, and ideas in these pages as you continue your ministry to black families. It will not be easy. But, as my mother would often say, anything worth having is worth working for. We might find strength in knowing that, in our commitment to minister to the multidimensional needs of black families in today's world, the presence of God is there to guide, sustain, heal, comfort, restore, and clarify our efforts and concerns, both in our local communities and beyond. Captured in the words of Paul's letter to the church of Philippi are indications of God's presence with believers in their service to God through others when he writes:

> Rejoice in the Lord always; again I will say, Rejoice.... Do not worry about anything, but in everything by prayer and supplication with thanksgiving let your requests be made known to God. And the peace of God, which surpasses all understanding, will guard your hearts and your minds in Christ Jesus. (Philippians 4:4-7, NRSV)

Let's get started!

CHAPTER 1

Grounded in Faith:
The Church and Black Family Life

JOHNNY B. HILL, PhD

*Honor your father and your mother, so that your days may
be long in the land that the* LORD *your God is giving you.*
(Exodus 20:12, NRSV)

The ruin of a nation begins in the homes of its people.
—Ashanti Ghana proverb

The strength of black family life is rooted in its resiliency and
spiritual creativity in confronting the joys and burdens of family. It is this sense of resiliency and faith, rooted in a history of
struggle, that holds the key to overcoming the problems facing
black families in today's world. In many ways, the relationship
between the church and black family in America are interwov-
en historical experiences. The experience of many African
Americans is not too foreign from that of Martin Luther King
Jr. As a child growing up on Auburn Avenue in Atlanta,
Georgia, King experienced the church as a second home.[1] For
many of us, to speak of the church means also to speak of family life. The black preacher in family life, for instance, was not

some lofty professional figure, but a very close member of an extended family network that stretched across biological and socioeconomic boundaries. Church and family went hand-in-hand in the black experience primarily because the church evolved into a stabilizing force when dramatic changes occurred. The church was the family for orphan children, widows and widowers, and the abused, neglected, downtrodden, and heartbroken. Indeed, for many African Americans, the family was the church and the church was the family. This theme was voiced in such passionate anonymous refrains as "Jesus has been mother to the motherless and father to the fatherless." The deep meaning of family and church has characterized the social and religious experience of blacks in its effort to fight off the dogs of dehumanization.

But how do we begin to recover that radical sense of harmony and interdependency between the family and the black church? What historical and theological resources are at our disposal as churches, individuals, and others who minister to black families? According to J. Deotis Roberts in *Roots of a Black Future: Black Family and Church*, it is imperative to explore more fully the *symbolic* and *actual* relationship between the family and church.[2] Roberts suggests the need for critical reflection on the meaning of church as family in terms of a paradigm for thinking about what it means to be the church. It is also important to examine the institutional importance of the relationship between family and church in the black experience. Many churches were established as either individual families or clusters of families coming together with the creative passion for fellowship, faith, and mutual sharing. Indeed, the church and the black family have been constant companions and have, in fact, modeled each other throughout history. The beauty and power of the black family may be attributed to this reality. By strengthening the family, the church, as well as the wider community, is also strengthened. As pastors, leaders, and congregations begin to think critically about how to meet the growing needs of families in their communities, one cannot deny the importance of faith, fellowship, and the promises of God, He is the author of family relationships, between sisters and brothers, parents and child, husband and wife, and even among the extended family as well.

God and Family

If the church is to be effective in ministry to black families, there must be a firm understanding of the church and its mission in the world. That the church is more than a social institution, but divinely inspired and directed, dictates the need for a sound theological position regarding the nature and mission of the church. Ministry to black families must be located in a theological framework that reflects the Christian gospel.

To fully understand the relationship between church and family, one simply needs to probe the historical experience of African American family life. The black family in America has never been the prototypical model based on Eurocentric standards. Since slavery the black family has taken on many forms. More often than not the black family has been characterized by relationships built on trust and interdependency and not necessarily on the commonly idealistic nuclear family unit of two heterosexual parents with children. On the contrary, black families have been defined by, and have lived by, the basis of their functionality.[3]

Throughout the Bible the concept of family is a persistent and recurring theme. It is the celebrated God of Israel who, through God's Son, invites humanity to participate in this divine family. At its most basic level in the nuclear family and expanded to all humans in the world, the human family is given the task to model the demonstrative love represented in the work of God in Christ. The contemporary theologian Jean Bethke Elshtain makes the important theological connection between family life in the *domus* (home) and what occurs in the *polis* (social and political public life).[4] By making the theological connection between family, the church, and society as a whole, we uproot the significance of family life in shaping the church and community.

The theme of the Holy Trinity (God the Father, Son, and Holy Spirit) carries deep theological meaning and insight into family life. In the divine love and creative energy (*perichoresis*) shared among the persons of the Trinity, human beings are given a powerful model and inspiration for what family looks like in our time. For instance, the relationship between God the Father and Jesus the Son suggests that real family relationship should be expressed in terms of sacramental and self-giving practices. In this sense, we see the family as more than a social institution where norms, rituals, and beliefs are developed, but as a divine organism inaugurated by God in Christ. For black families, understanding God as one who sustains, heals, transforms, and reconciles broken relationships can provide tremendous resources for overcoming the internal and external forces militating against black family life. The unlimited, self-generating, self-perpetuating love of God in Christ, through the Holy Spirit, is especially meaningful in light of various dimensions and challenges inherent in black family life.

Biblical Images of Family

Not all families look the same. We must resist the urge to place all families in a box and force families to conform to one image. The Scriptures are full of many different examples and configurations of family. Family, in the biblical sense, is defined by a covenantal relationship, not a biological one. Five biblical examples of family models come to mind: the stories of Hagar, Moses, Ruth and Naomi, Joseph and Mary, and the apostle Paul. In each of these experiences, they share a different understanding of who their family was and what it meant to be family.

Hagar

The biblical story of Hagar depicts a servant woman who was given to Abraham by his wife, Sarah, as a surrogate mother (see Genesis 16 and 21). Rejected by Sarah, Abraham's first wife, Hagar was exiled to the wilderness with her young son, Ishmael. In modern-day language, Hagar was forced to become a "single parent." God sent an angel to direct Hagar to needed resources for her crying child. The story reveals God's deep love and concern for all families and all individuals.

The Hagar story uncovers the ways in which God's vision of family is not limited to the modern Americanized notion of a nuclear family unit consisting of a husband-wife couple with children and a dog. On the contrary, in human history, families have always taken on diverse forms. Considering the fact that an overwhelming majority of black households are single-parent led, the story of Hagar comes as comfort and assurance that God celebrates and affirms God's love for families that resembles Hagar's experience.

Moses

Moses presents a different biblical model of a family used by God (see Exodus 2). Under threat of death, Moses was surrendered in infancy by his biological family and adopted by the Egyptian royal family. He grew up in a highly privileged environment, but his real identity was hidden from him until he became an adult. As the story goes, Moses escaped his "homeland" of Egypt and was "adopted" again—this time by marriage into a nomadic clan in Midian. Although Moses is often cast as an Old Testament messianic figure and deliverer, his model of family would be what some might call "dysfunctional."

By "dysfunctional," I mean the problematic labels placed on families that somehow fall short of the idealized understanding of family recognized by many social service agencies. From God's perspective, there is no such thing as a dysfunctional family. Rather, as Moses reveals, through God's grace, protection, and divine presence, individuals and families have the capacity to thrive as they seek to live out God's purpose in their lives. There is no evidence that Moses actually knew who his real father was. He was estranged from his birth family and heritage. Even after he fled from Egypt to live among the Midianites, he became a stranger in a strange land.

From Moses, we also find a biblical model of family that integrates the complexities of both formal and informal adoptions in the black community. One of the unique characteristics of the black family that scholars such as Robert Hill and Andrew Billingsley have pointed out is that informal adoptions are particularly common occurrences for many. For instance, in many black families, we see siblings, uncles, aunts, or grandparents take on parental responsibilities when a parent is deemed unwilling or incapable. This could be voluntary or involuntary. In either case, the strong communal character of black family life in the quest for survival reflects much of the same dynamics at work in the story of Moses as well.

Ruth and Naomi

The story of Ruth and Naomi offers further illustrations of God's vision of family as broad and all inclusive (see the book of Ruth). Naomi's "traditional" family of husband and children is decimated, to be replaced by a household of two women devoted to one another with no biological or surviving legal ties. Eventually, that model of family is expanded as well when the widowed Ruth marries again and produces a child who is largely raised by his honorary grandmother.

An overlooked population in many black churches is families made up of siblings or family members as part of the sandwich generation who are providing support for aging relatives. Many widows, orphans, close friends, or displaced persons find themselves gravitating to create family support systems. These individuals and relationships also need to be acknowledged and celebrated as the church reflects on its vision and scope of family ministry. As is evident in the story of Ruth and Naomi, God works in and through a diverse configuration of relational ties. The story demonstrates that ultimately what defines family in the life of God are relationality and fellowship. The relationships we share with those most dear to us, whether they are kinship ties or intentionally created bonds, constitute an important aspect of a faithful approach to family from the biblical perspective. It would be irresponsible to limit one's view of family to a singular makeup. Because all of us, particularly believers, live within a complex web of interconnectedness, we are called to broaden our understanding of family. Briefly considering the story of Ruth and her relationship with Naomi merely provides one way of doing just that.

Joseph and Mary

Of course, while there are many examples of family in Scripture that would not ordinarily be consistent with the traditional notion of family, the witness of Mary and Joseph as Luke describes in his gospel is such a case. The story of Joseph and Mary continues to be a mainstay for Easter plays and festive events in church, but very rarely have churches, theologians, or even preachers looked to Joseph and Mary as a model for family. One can understand the reluctance. After all, Mary was under-age, and because he suspected her of unfaithfulness, Joseph came close to breaking off the engagement. Their story is not exactly what some would consider an ideal relationship! However, in spite of the obvious challenges, Joseph and Mary provide resources for considering the ways in which it is God's desire for both mother and father to create a loving and nurturing atmosphere in which children may grow and develop. In addition to providing loving companionship to each other, Joseph and Mary were called to allow their mutual love and concern as spouses to be projected toward their son Jesus. The healthy and vibrant formation of Jesus as he prepared to walk in his identity as the Messiah was due in part to the parental and familial faithfulness of his earthly parents. Joseph and Mary provide a wonderful model of family insofar as their capacity for loving each other and Jesus was not a consequence of their material well-being, but their reliance on each other and on God. Through the Holy Spirit, Mary and Joseph found strength, guidance, and clarity in a purposeful walk with each other and God.

Paul

The apostle Paul is yet another model of the biblical family because that great teacher and church planter advocated (and presumably lived) a single life for most, if not all, of his adult years. He even recommended it as a preferred family model for those dedicated to ministry, and talked about the church as an extended family—the family of God into which we all are adopted.

A growing number of believers are choosing to lead both a celibate and single lifestyle that should not only be valued but also viewed as a legitimate expression of Christian living. I think most of us who have actively participated in black church settings have observed that a common temptation is for the community to play matchmaker. That is, there is often an unspoken perspective that a single person is somehow incomplete, in need of a heterosexual mate for wholeness. However, through the writings of Paul, we see a confident, Spirit-filled, focused, and intelligent person who understands the church as family and family as church. What Paul's life reveals is that there are incredible resources within the church for developing deep and authentic relationships and finding community in ways that may not otherwise be available. A comprehensive approach to ministry in black churches must be intentional about integrating single individuals and those who choose to live alone into its ministry's mission.

We might find courage and comfort in knowing that, in God's sight, there is no such thing as a perfect earthly family. Biblical stories give us insight into God's perspective that developing meaningful and loving covenant relationships centered on God are essential to the meaning and definition of family.

Strategies That Work

As the reader will find throughout this book, there are many churches, faith-based organizations, and other institutions that have developed effective strategies with proven results in their ministry to black families. There are several characteristics of successful and faithful programs that churches in particular will find essential. They include:

■ a holistic approach that considers the spiritual, emotional, and economic needs of the family
■ serious and intentional education or instructional commitments to all members of a particular family
■ spiritual formation opportunities and pastoral support
■ long-term follow-up and continual nurturing of the family

Let's look at some ways to implement these characteristics.

Thinking Holistically

Any ministry to families must take into account that individuals and families are not simply sociological constructs, but spiritual organisms situated in a material world. Too often in churches there has been an inexorable amount of emphasis on spirituality with no thoughtful consideration to a family's economic well-being. Conversely, some churches have focused solely on the physical dimensions of family life and have neglected the spiritual development of the family as it relates to faith, healing, forgiveness, and reconciliation. A meaningful balance, in a holistic sense, will make a lasting difference in the life of black families of all configurations.

Building Partnerships and Teams

A holistic approach to black family ministry is more than a notion. It embodies the arduous task of partnerships and team building. Most African American congregations are accustomed to the pastor-centered model of ministry. Pastors are often called upon to meet every need of families and individuals, ranging from counseling and social work to financial advisement and health advocacy.

Whether this way of viewing ministry came into being because pastors enjoyed the position of dependency and importance or simply because of the overwhelmingly diverse demands of black family life, today's ministry to families calls for partnership, networking, and committed teamwork. Churches and leaders must seek ways to connect with existing organizations, while also seizing upon the wealth of gifts and talents available in the pews. In a post–civil rights world, there is a sizable population of Christians in most congregations who are psychologists, bankers, real estate agents, scientists, entrepreneurs, and more. But the challenge arises when believers attempt to integrate their "secular" knowledge and training in the life of the church. We must begin to deconstruct the notion that there are realms of knowledge and experience that may have value outside the church but seem to be of no value within the ecclesiastical corridors.

The apostle Paul, in his own appropriation of Greek philosophy and language to illuminate the gospel, declared, "We know that in all things God works for the good of those who love him, who have been called according to his purpose" (Romans 8:28, NIV). In this Romans text, the apostle was speaking to the struggle of the Christian life in a fallen world. As he confronted the bitter reality of sin and suffering amid the affirmation of the resurrection of Jesus, Paul made it resoundingly clear that Christian practice does not come without incredible cost and sacrifice. Paul tells us that the Christian life is a life of struggle, but that hope lies in the glory of God in Christ. In seeking partnerships and teamwork, the Christian language centering on the work of God in Christ collapses the distinctions often made in terms of what is "sacred" and "secular." Overall, the unifying force in the church's ministry to black families is rooted in Christian community. Centered on the person of Christ, pastors, churches, lay leaders, and others must therefore be intentional about forming partnerships and teams to address the multidimensional challenges facing black family life.

Providing Intentional Christian Education to Families

Along with an intentional focus on team building and partnerships, ministry to black families also requires careful reflection on education and instruction. Churches must go beyond merely a "Sunday school" approach to Christian education, especially as it relates to black families. By that I mean church leaders must carve out the creative space for serious, transparent, and public dialogue on the problems that affect black family life. Issues such as housing, unemployment, neglect, domestic violence, and drug abuse are normal occurrences but often remain hidden behind the veil of religious and cultural superficiality. In an effort to conform to the enormous pressure to have it all together and appear spiritually and materially prosperous in church settings, the deep and intrinsic problems of the black family go undetected.

Offering educational and instructional opportunities means integrating the centrality of ministry to families into the very fabric of the church's mission. This commitment must be reflected in the church's budget and hiring practices as well. Ministry to family that is holistic incorporates youth, parents, guardians, siblings, mentors, teachers, and other important relational connections, and must not simply be a sidebar discussion. As churches begin to educate and teach, not simply to individuals but to families as well, they lead a process of healing, transformation, and resiliency.

Christian education opportunities are usually very compartmentalized based on gender, age, interest, marital status, and the like. While these distinctions are very essential, and there is much need to treat the individual spiritual development of believers, this approach alone can often lead to a fractured understanding of some of the root causes of brokenness, which can often be traced to familial connections. Simply expanding the particular nature of Christian education and instruction to include workshops, talks, courses, even sermons that address the whole family (not just individuals) is an important step toward building stronger family units.

Partnerships and Christian educational opportunities would have little to no lasting effect without some attention to spiritual formation and ongoing support and nurturing. One of the strategies many churches are employing to minister to the entire family is to develop small group or "cell" ministries organized by "households" or families in a particular geographic area. In Willow Creek Church in Barrington, Illinois, this approach has had very positive results, in part because while large gatherings can be quite intimidating, small groups create the space for intimate sharing and the context for meaningful relationship building. Also, members of a particular family who perhaps would not usually attend a function held on church grounds might find a small group environment in a home setting more inviting. Spiritual formation among families can take on other expressions as well, such as faith-centered family reunions, house blessings, family celebrations for weddings, anniversaries, birthdays, promotions, and so on. The idea that spiritual formation should be viewed in the context of family life poses a significant challenge to the entrenched culture of individualism.

Spiritual formation has traditionally taken the form of individual pietistic development. By that I mean that both in the past and present, the church has been preoccupied with thinking about the individual's spiritual needs. Certainly reflecting on individual spirituality is essential; however, individual spirituality would be incomplete without taking into consideration other family, extended family, and significant relationships in shaping spiritual outlook. Indeed, not only are we individuals but we are persons in community as well. When pastors, churches, lay leaders, and teachers seek to minister to a particular individual, it is critical to also find ways to connect with family. For instance, praying with the individual and the family, considering important relationships in the life of an individual, and seeking to establish a community of support and spiritual accountability are ways of connecting a sense of communal spirituality with the process of spiritual formation and growth.

Providing Long-term Nurturing and Follow-up

The final theme that is immutable in ministry to black families is continual nurturing and long-term follow-up. Christian believers, by their very nature, are idealistic and excited about the prospects of making a creative and meaningful difference in the life of others. There is something extremely intriguing about participating in God's ministry of transformation, healing, restoration, and reconciliation when it comes to black family life. The challenge, however, arises during the difficult period after the initial attempts of working with families has waned. Some follow-up plan is therefore essential for successful ministry to take root and grow.

There are no quick-fix solutions to the complex problems facing black family life. Nevertheless, there is room to celebrate the fact that many families continue to thrive and contribute greatly to their church and wider community. By engaging in meaningful and honest conversations about the problems that do exist, churches and families are well on their way to making a powerful difference in their communities.

NOTES

1. Carson Clayborne, *The Papers of Martin Luther King, Jr.* (1956–64), vol. 1, (Berkeley: University of California Press, 1992), 30.

2. J. Deotis Roberts, *Roots of a Black Future: Black Family and Church* (Bowie, MD: J. Deotis Roberts Press, 2002), 1.

3. Robert Bernard Hill, *The Strengths of African American Families: Twenty-Five Years Later* (Baltimore: University Press of America, 1999), 6ff.

4. Jean Bethke Elshtain, *Augustine and the Limits of Politics* (Notre Dame, IN: University of Notre Dame Press, 1995), n.p.

CHAPTER 2

Elephants in the Pews: Confronting Silent Issues in the Church

SHERRILL McMILLAN, MD

What the church doesn't talk about is acted out in the pews and the pulpit. And talk without intervention too quickly turns into gossip which guarantees that many worshippers will leave church services week after week with the same issues and problems of life as when they entered. We're at a point in the life of the local church that demands we begin to take an active role in confronting the elephants in the room. Historically the church has successfully ignored domestic violence, denied alcoholism and drug addiction, justified adultery, demonized human sexuality, blamed HIV/AIDS and down-low-ism on the homosexual and bisexual population, and turned its head away from blatant fornication among heterosexuals.

The separation and divorce rate among the Christian community closely parallels the secular statistics, due in large part to persons getting married when they shouldn't and to persons with whom they should have just remained friends. And because we don't fully understand emotional disorders and mental illness, the church has isolated and mistreated its suffering members. These members are simply acting out a disorder for which we could be very helpful, if only we would.

One of the ways churches can confront this silence is by developing comprehensive counseling and support centers that uphold the Christian faith as well as family systems theory and practice. By working collaboratively with trained mental health professionals and people of faith, we can establish conditions to begin to open up dialogue. Classic family systems theory and practice suggests that each person is a product of early childhood learning and experiences. If we are brave enough to go back in time over three generations and make an honest assessment of our family values, ethics, and patterns of behavior, it soon becomes evident that we inherit our patterns of cognition and behavior from what we have seen and learned in our own family systems. From this perspective, the iniquity of the parents is visited "upon the children and the children's children, to the third and fourth generation" (Exodus 34:7, NRSV). Just as we inherit the genes for hypertension, diabetes, and heart disease, we also inherit our models for interpersonal relationships, addictions, sexual ethics, domestic violence, and a host of maladaptive behaviors that contribute to the moral and ethical decline of the family. Confessing our faults to one another and praying for the healing of our brothers and sisters in Christ (James 5:16, NRSV) is one of the biblical models for dealing with elephants in the room.

However, public confession becomes increasingly more difficult as we climb the church ladder to the pulpit and other leadership roles where the expectation is that the illnesses common to man do not affect those who have been placed on such high and holy pedestals. African Americans have historically looked to the church for help and guidance in times of personal and family stress. But when the church can't be trusted to keep the secrets of the abused and misused, it only adds to the silent suffering. If the church can't intervene in the lives of those struggling with emotional wounds, psychological stress, and mental illness without fear and contempt, then the elephants are running rampant in the room and we are all in danger of spiritual stampede.

The challenge for the church is to break the silence of those dark places in the life of God's people that impair our Christian growth and the growth of the local church body. What we don't talk about, we act out. Or we talk about our issues in such vague and safe ways that the issues appear almost nonexistent.

It's easy to generalize marriage problems, but to say that many Christian marriages are marked by emotional and physical abuse is the painful truth. There are other painful truths to consider as well. These are just a few scenarios:

■ We admit that adultery is no stranger to the Christian community. It is one thing to find your wife in bed with another man. It's a different matter, however, to find her in bed with another woman. The down-low is no joke!

■ The saints among us are quick to pull out an aspirin or Tylenol bottle in public but wouldn't dare pull out the bottle of alcohol or the illegal drug that has rendered them an addict.

■ Family members continue to say to the public that their son or daughter died of a rare blood disorder rather than admit the child died of AIDS. They weren't able to break the silence in life, and they are unable to break it in death.

■ The saints among us are quick to seek medical attention for hypertension and diabetes and often brag about the number and kinds of medications they take daily. But fear and ignorance keep them silent about psychological illnesses that are just as debilitating and for which there are therapeutic interventions that can help them avoid long-term care or institutionalization.

■ And perhaps the pulpits and ministerial pews in our churches harbor some of the best-kept secrets in the Christian community. Preachers and pastors and ministry leaders have marital, health, or substance abuse issues that are often intensified by the very nature of their ministry.

Since 1948 The World Health Organization has defined health as a "state of complete physical, mental and social well-being and not merely the absence of disease or infirmity." Few, if any, of us can meet such strict criteria for being healthy by this definition. *The American Journal of Health Promotion* (1989) offers the more realistic definition of optimal health as "a balance of physical, emotional, social, spiritual and intellectual health." Perhaps it is even more practical to view health on a continuum that represents the severity of issues from few health concerns to serious health issues, minimal psychological issues to serious clinical diagnoses, low tension to high stress, learned anger management to family violence, moderate drug consumption to substance abuse, and that has a solid spiritual foundation at one end and the equivalent of sinking sand at the other end.

The Hidden Epidemics: STDs, HIV, and Domestic Violence

God was not being punitive when he commanded us to abstain from sex before marriage. Neither was he anything less than serious when he instructed us to "let marriage be held in honor by all, and let the marriage bed be kept undefiled; for God will judge fornicators and adulterers" (Hebrews 13:4, NRSV). God's discipline and judgment are always for our benefit, and his intentions are that we should learn from the consequences of our mistakes and disobedience. The fact that sexually transmitted diseases (STDs) have reached epidemic proportions in the African American community is no secret. What is kept secret, however, by the thousands of men and women in the faith community is that sexual behavior has not significantly changed in spite of the warnings and evidence of the danger of operating outside of God's law. Single men and women have convinced themselves that they are being sexually responsible because they test for STDs, HIV, and AIDS every six months.

The problem with this line of thinking is that the statement itself shows they have not been responsible enough to change their behavior; they merely test until they come up positive! A positive HIV diagnosis may no longer be the automatic death sentence it was in years past; nevertheless, it is life altering. The situation is made worse by men and women who intentionally contribute to the epidemic by having sex with full knowledge of their positive status without telling their partners. The sadder commentary is that Christian men and women resist the fact that sexual abstinence is the only guaranteed way of preventing diseases caused by sexual activity. We profess to be filled with the Spirit of God but act out in the flesh in such a way that the lust of the flesh overrides the control of the Spirit.

As recently as 2002, the Centers for Disease Control reported that HIV/AIDS was the second leading cause of death for all African Americans ages 35–44 and HIV/AIDS was the number one cause of death for African American women ages 25–34. In 2004, out of the more than 38,000 cases of HIV/AIDS diagnosed, 50 percent were African American. Gonorrhea rates were 30 times higher in African Americans than in whites, and African American women were at high risk for genital herpes. And these diseases are preventable.

The rising numbers of STDs and HIV cases among adolescents is alarming and, with few exceptions, the church is still silent on this issue and avoids the much needed preaching, teaching, and witnessing about sexual behaviors and the negative impact of fornication and adultery. Much of this problem seems to stem from the fact that some of the perpetrators are the very leaders who are called to set the examples. When our young people witness adulterous marriages, observe women pregnant out of wedlock, and are exposed to young and old men who have no problem talking about the notches on their belts, the message of God stands in stark contradiction to the messengers.

Domestic violence is the other social epidemic that is hidden in the pews. Since all violence is not physical, there are women and men among us who bear emotional scars that sometimes last longer than physical scars. Victims of physical and emotional abuse are fearful of seeking help from the church because of the stigmas attached to domestic violence and the fear that confidentiality will be quickly violated, causing victims to lose their anonymity. Violence against women by perpetrators who have learned maladaptive behaviors is reflective of systemic trauma and dysfunction that have transformed intangibles such as power and control into tangible acts of violence against women: scars, burns, bruises, and broken bones. Images of abused women are often of those who are young, poor, underprivileged, uneducated—women who have limited or nonexistent family and economic support. *The Legal Momentum* (2006) reports that as many as 60 percent of female welfare recipients have been victims of domestic violence and that many of these welfare recipients were also victims of physical or sexual abuse as children. The larger picture, however, supports the fact that victims of abuse are also doctors, lawyers, teachers, preachers, Sunday school teachers, and clergy wives and husbands.

Child abuse and neglect are also among the best kept secrets in local congregations. Perpetrators of violence and victims of violence were mostly likely abused or exposed to abuse as children. The biology of child abuse is the subject of a 2005 report by Harvard Medical School, which states: "Apart from heredity and recent stress, child maltreatment is the most common predictor of major depression in adults. People who suffer childhood maltreatment are more vulnerable to post-traumatic stress because their bodies have learned that they cannot count on protection and solace in distressing situations." The body and brain learn to adapt to the stress of victimization, and high levels of stress hormones over the long-term affect the body's ability to physically or psychologically relax. It is not uncommon for victims of abuse to feel nervous and anxious for a good part of each day. Children and adults have learned that it's not safe to let their guard down, subjecting them to constant emotional pressure over the course of time. Traumatic experiences are stored in long-term memory, and these experiences are easily brought into current thought by any situation that remotely reminds the victim of prior trauma.

Victims of abuse often react to behaviors that nonvictims

wouldn't consider threatening. For instance, a sudden change in voice tone or escalation in volume, an abrupt nonverbal behavior such as raising a hand, or a sudden change of facial expressions during what might be considered a casual conversation may remind the victim of a prior negative experience sufficiently to produce fear. Flashbacks are often accompanied by a rise in blood pressure and blood sugar and an increase in heart rate. Victims of abuse are likely to experience the same tension and fear as if the abuse happened yesterday. And for many it indeed did happen yesterday. These victims also suffer spiritually. It is not uncommon for female victims of abuse by men to have difficulty relating to God as Father because of their memories of malicious treatment by their own fathers, stepfathers, and other father figures. Adult female victims of childhood abuse often experience lingering sexual difficulties with their spouses; have erroneously learned to use sex in an attempt to gain approval from men; are likely to overspend to fulfill delayed gratification from childhood and, consequently, have severe financial difficulties as adults; are prone to suicidal tendencies that are kept secret; and are challenged by physical injuries or diseases as a result of childhood and adult sexual abuse.

The sexual abuse of women remains another problem that is not talked about in healthy ways at the local church level. Reporting rape to legal authorities still poses a serious challenge for women because they fear having their sexual histories tried in a court of law. It is a continuing challenge for a woman to prove that her husband has raped her, and acquaintance rape or date rape is a growing concern among adolescents and young adults. Teenagers are especially reluctant to tell adults about date rape for fear they will somehow be blamed for the assault or that they will continually have to face a male perpetrator who may go unpunished. Dr. Christina Sommers cites "Sexual Experiences Survey," the 1982 study by Mary Koss at Kent State University, which described rape as normal male behavior consistent with the male dominant ideology of our culture. Koss's 1982 study of more than 3,000 students found that one in every four women had been victims of rape or attempted rape; 84 percent of the victims knew their attacker; 57 percent of the victims were raped while on a date; 42 percent of the victims did not disclose that they had been raped; and 84 percent of the men who committed rape did not consider themselves as having raped their victims.

Rape is seldom, if ever, about sex; it is more about power and control, and often the victim is unaware that the perpetrator has a plan for abusing the relationship. A woman is further reluctant to report sexual assault out of fear of being blamed for encouraging the assault or setting up a sexual encounter and then changing her mind. What was she wearing? What did she do to lead him on? What was she doing with him in the first place? Had she had sex with him before? None of these questions have anything to do with the fact that a violent crime has been committed against the victim's will. *No* means no. For many African American victims of rape, a woman has to prove not only that she was raped but that, as a black woman, she is even capable of being raped. The laws of racial discrimination are still on the silent pages of time, and the stereotype that black women are more promiscuous is as erroneous now as it was during slavery. The slaves somehow managed to prohibit interracial sex but not interracial rape.

A Mind Is a Terrible Thing to Ignore

Our emotional and psychological conditions are described in two books: the Bible, and the *Diagnostic and Statistical Manual of Mental Disorders* published by the American Psychiatric Association. We don't escape emotional or psychological problems because we are Christians. Rather, it is the very nature of sin to affect us in adverse ways. Some of our psychological issues are genetic, some are the result of environmental stressors, and some are caused by our own errors in judgment and mistreatment of our bodies. Because we all are affected by sin, we all have issues. But it takes less courage to point a finger at someone else's sin than to acknowledge our own. "Why do you see the speck in your neighbor's eye, but do not notice the log in your own eye?" (Luke 6:41, NRSV) This question that Jesus asked begs the issue of self-righteousness, but as long as we keep the spotlight on someone else, it keeps us in the dark about our own mental condition.

The stigma of mental illness, especially among the black community, is still so great that we'd rather have a terminal illness in our bodies than to own up to depression, anxiety, bipolar disorder, schizophrenia, alcoholism or drug addiction, gambling disorders, sexual addictions, or any of the diagnoses that label us "different" from those who are considered to be "normal." However, the term *normal* is a misnomer and one that is relative to time, place, person, and situation. We all fall short of the normal mark, and it is common for many adults to spend too much time trying to be normal and not enough time trying to be well. Wellness is a holistic term that applies to the physical body, the mind, and our spiritual condition, and there is an intrinsic relationship between all three components. The average person who was diagnosed with high blood pressure or diabetes would not dare ignore this condition, but would take care in making regular doctor's visits and taking the prescribed medications. But we take huge chances by ignoring the symptoms of psychological stress and mental illness when, in the final analysis, the mind might be the only thing we have left to get us through this life.

In the last fifteen years, we've had to intervene on behalf of African Americans with psychological disorders we've never had to pay attention to before, mostly because the community ignores all the symptoms and waits until the only way to treat them is with medication or institutionalization. Too often it's too little too late. What might have been just a temporary challenge often turns into a permanent setback. Fear and the stigma of mental illness as well as the church's resistance to healing by means other than prayer and fasting, have kept us from taking advantage of what God has provided for our healing. The resistance and the hesitancy are understandable from a historical perspective. There was a time when we were not blessed with mental health professionals and paraprofessionals in the African American community. But today there are many who are trained in counseling, psychology, and theology and who know something about confidentiality. It's time to take advantage of these resources in our church community.

The Possibilities of Christian Counseling

God has made amazing provisions for our mental health by providing us with psychologists, family therapists, social workers, professional counselors, and others in the mental health disciplines who have been trained in psychological theory and practice and in the spiritual applications of the Word of God. Christian counseling has, as its base, a biblical worldview and a high Christology. We are guided by the Holy Spirit in examining the relationship between sin and psychopathology, and we view therapy as Godly activity as we seek to impart the reign of God into human transformation. Sin has affected every part of our being, and our mental condition is no exception. Psychological stress and mental illness are not sins to be forgiven but conditions to be treated by professionals whom God has placed among us for our mental and spiritual wellness.

If we really believe that the local church is a hospital for the sick, then we should not be surprised when sick people show up. Some show up with hypertension, some show up blind, some show up in need of spiritual development, and some show up with emotional frailties and psychological disorders. Some people are difficult, manipulative, jealous, rebellious, and mean. Others appear anxious, or depressed, or their speech is scattered and incoherent. Some exhibit what we label strange behavior because they are experiencing severe mental distress that may cause them to appear strange to those who see themselves as normal. Ezekiel lay on his left side for 390 days, shaved his head with a sword, and weighed the strands (Ezekiel 4:1-8; 5:1), all at God's request. How strange is that? As much as David was loved by God, he was still an adulterer; Saul needed the music of David's harp to soothe his depressive episodes; Noah couldn't keep his hands off the bottle; Moses had murder in his heart that he acted out; Jacob was a manipulator; and Jezebel and Delilah have given women a bad name for centuries. But there was a plan of God and a lesson for the people of God in each of these cases.

We all have issues, and our issues are in the Bible and in the *Diagnostic and Statistical Manual of Mental Disorders*. Failure to acknowledge one or both of those resources is what causes Christians to want to hide behind their mental challenges, point fingers in the wrong direction, and allow conditions that can be managed to get out of control until they put the spiritual health of the church at risk. Mental illness is not a sin. Jesus healed a diversity of afflictions of the body and the mind. At one end of the spectrum he dispelled the notion that affliction was caused by sin (John 9:1-3) while at the other end of that same spectrum, he warned the lame man to take care not to sin again so that nothing worse would fall upon him (John 5:14). These two passages are not contradictory. Rather, they give us two different insights into the source and cause of our afflictions. One source may well be genetics since we now know that some of us carry genes for a predisposition to certain types of depressive disorders, for example. Role models from our families of origin may be the source of certain addictive behaviors in children and adults. Other sources of our mental conditions derive from stress and emotional turmoil resulting from our mistakes, errors in judgment about the relationships we enter into, or financial decisions we make and live to regret.

Let the Church Say "Amen"

The remedy for many of these challenges is in our midst. God has placed capable mental health professionals in the local church as a gift to the body. Many churches have acted on the necessity of incorporating mental health and counseling centers as nonprofit affiliates of the local church to minister to the needs of persons with psychological and psychosocial challenges. Other churches have also trained and used paraprofessionals to assist in their work.

The Garment's Hem, Inc., is a nonprofit affiliate of the Metropolitan Baptist Church in Washington, DC, and employs a group of licensed professionals who provide medical and mental health services in the Washington metropolitan area and beyond. Located in Prince Georges County, Maryland, the nonprofit component began as a peer counseling ministry of the church in the early 1990s and has grown into a professional agency. Their services include the following:

■ individual, couples, and family therapy
■ parent-child conflict resolution
■ grief and loss counseling
■ mental health assessment
■ premarital workshops
■ community health awareness fairs
■ health and dental screenings for children and adults
■ fitness and body mass index assessments
■ community workshops for churches and schools

The Garment's Hem provides annual child abuse prevention and intervention training for all staff members and volunteers of the church who work with children and adolescents. Volunteers and staff are only eligible to work with children and youth after they have successfully cleared a criminal background check and meet the annual continuing education requirements.

Paraprofessionals are trained to provide low-cost and pro bono counseling services to individuals and families in the church. Paraprofessionals are required to complete a ten-month training program that includes legal and ethical issues, including confidentiality and duty to warn; basic counseling techniques; and a practicum experience. Licensed professionals provide continuing education for paraprofessionals several times annually. Paraprofessional counselors are assigned to the emergency response team, which is comprised of medical and mental health personnel who provide crises response services as needed for congregants during scheduled worship services.

There may be elephants in the pews, but the good news is that God has made provision for our physical, mental, and spiritual health. We need not be injured by the stampede.

References

American Journal of Health Promotion, 3 no. 3 (1989): 5.

"The Biology of Child Maltreatment." *Harvard Mental Health Letter* 21, no. 12 (June 2005): 1–20.

Centers for Disease Control and Prevention (2006). HIV/AIDS Prevention. www.cdc.gov/hiv/topics/aa.

Consumer Health Foundation (2005). Annual Report. Washington, DC.

Diagnostic and Statistical Manual of Mental Disorders, 4th ed. (Washington, DC: American Psychiatric Association, 1994).

Koss, Mary, and Cheryl Oros. "Sexual Experiences Survey: A Research Instrument Investigating Sexual Aggression and Victimization," *Journal of Consulting and Clinical Psychology* 50, no. 3 (1982): 455.

Mullholland, A. M., and L. B. Mintz. "Prevalence of Eating Disorders among African American Women." *Journal of Counseling Psychology* 48 (2001): 111–16.

Pike, K. M., F. A. Dohm, R. H. Striegel-Moore, D. E. Wilfley, and C. G. Fairburn. "A Comparison of Black and White Women with Binge Eating Disorders," in *American Journal of Psychiatry* 158, no. 9 (2001): 1455–60.

Sommers, Christina. *One Nation under Therapy: How Helping Culture Is Eroding Self-Reliance* (New York: St. Martin's, 2005).

CHAPTER 3

Gettin' Ready to Jump da Broom and How to Make Your Good Thing Better!

LORRAINE C. BLACKMAN, PhD, LCSW, CFLE

The Spirit of the Sovereign LORD is on me,
because the LORD has anointed me
to preach good news to the poor.
He has sent me to bind up the brokenhearted,
to proclaim freedom for the captives
and release from darkness for the prisoners,
to proclaim the year of the LORD's favor
and the day of vengeance of our God,
to comfort all who mourn,
and provide for those who grieve in Zion—
to bestow on them a crown of beauty
instead of ashes, the oil of gladness
instead of mourning, and a garment of praise
instead of a spirit of despair. (Isaiah 61:1-3, NIV)

Despite the obvious problems of poverty, incarceration, and sadness among families in their congregations, one of the most difficult topics for contemporary black churches to tackle is that of the quality of family life. In particular, the foundational institution of marriage is difficult to broach.

Only about one-third of black households are headed by married couples. The proportion of cohabiting couples, even among church attendees, has skyrocketed over the past forty years, and approximately 75 percent of black children are born to unwed parents. Nearly 25 percent of black households fall below the federal poverty guidelines, but the rate for households with minor children exceeds 33 percent. That rate soars above 49 percent in families with children and a female head of household.[1]

Nonetheless, the topic of family life, and especially marriage, against this statistical backdrop is difficult because if one looks out at most black congregations, 70 percent of attendees are women who have never married or are divorced or widowed. Then there are girls and boys, mostly under the age of 12, who have never lived in a two-spouse headed household. If there are men present in the congregation, most are over age fifty and from a generation when public dialogue about "private, family matters," especially sexual ones, were not discussed—certainly not at church! There is a noticeable absence of males ages 12–49.

Church leaders, hesitant to offend or alienate congregants, tread cautiously around these matters. "Most churches express awareness of the need for holistic family ministry, yet few make adequate investments to equip the church to address the rising trend of brokenness experienced by the African American family."[2]

The congregational picture is distressing, particularly since it mirrors that of most black households—that is, women and children living apart from husbands and fathers. Additionally, men and women, particularly those under age thirty, frequently have children with multiple partners who are increasingly from other racial or ethnic groups. They refer to each other, in the hip-hop vernacular, as "my baby's mamma or daddy." As required by the welfare reform legislation of 1996,[3] these parents flood the courts across the nation—including those on television—in efforts to establish the paternity of children and to secure child support and visitation. Yet even when couples marry, 48 percent of all marriages end in divorce.[4] Unfortunately, these patterns of unstable intimate relationships and parenting are no different for church attendees than for nonchurchgoers.

Furthermore, the research literature makes it clear that problems such as poor school performance, juvenile delinquency, drug abuse, homicide, suicide, out-of-wedlock pregnancies, and sexually transmitted diseases, such as HIV/AIDS, are often tied to the absence of fathers in the homes and lives of children.[5] Among dating teenagers, 20 percent of female high school students report experiencing intimidation or violence by their boyfriends.[6] Approximately 35 percent of births are to unmarried women age 15 and older, and most to women with a high school education or less.[7] More than 21,000 new HIV/AIDS cases among blacks were diagnosed in 2003, most among ages 25–54, but almost 2,000 were as young as 15–24 years old, and approximately 3,000 were 55–64 years of age. Forty-nine percent (49%) were males and 51 percent were females.[8] Female cases were most often related to having heterosexual relations with men who had sex with other men (MSM), also known as "brothers on the down-low." Among men the predominant source is MSM.[9] In 2004, 21 percent of all deaths among blacks were attributable to AIDS.

Given these daunting statistics on black family life, what is needed is a substantial increase in the numbers of godly men and women as teaching parents, loving spouses, and divinely inspired leaders in their homes. Often in an effort to avoid offending single mothers, clergy and church leaders send the message that families can function without men as fathers and husbands. However, statistics testify that men, women, and children are happier, healthier, and more successful when their dreams of healthy family life come true. "[Research] findings do indicate the importance of a combination of both satisfying intimate relations [i.e., family life, broken, or unbroken marriages] and personal achievement for overall life satisfaction."[10]

As I reflect on my own father, I recall a tall, quiet, handsome man wearing thick glasses, a man whose primary aim in life was to ensure the economic well-being and safety of both his family of origin and his family of creation. His divorced mother and four siblings relied heavily on him from age 9 until his death from cancer at age 57. In addition, from the time he was 20 years old, his young wife and two children could count on his diligence to improve steadily their quality of life, both materially and spiritually. Despite their enormous responsibilities, my working parents found time to nurture each other, my brother and me, extended kin, church members, and many friends. Each also mentored young men and women along the way; my mother still does. They were not materially wealthy, but each created a lasting legacy of love. We need millions more godly men and women who will do the same for present and future generations.

That is why it is vitally important for churches to promote healthy marriage and to teach men and women how to achieve it. This teaching requires much knowledge, skill, and sensitivity on the part of clergy and lay leaders who dare tread into these turbulent waters. The following critical research, anecdotal evidence, and practical step-by-step guides will provide clergy and congregations with more insight into the various resources available to black churches in preparing people for marriage. The goal, beginning in childhood, is to teach individuals how to create and maintain strong, healthy marriages and families. Beginning with children might seem awkward to some, but a rationale and model for developing teaching materials and approaches in the black church might be found in the Latter-day Saints' approach to the process:

> God expects parents in the Church to teach their children about procreation and chastity and to prepare

them for dating and marriage. This responsibility should not be left to schools, friends, playmates, or strangers. Heavenly Father wishes his children to understand how to use this great and holy power wisely and reverently. If parents will seek the guidance of the Spirit in humble prayer, he will help them teach their children about this sacred power.[11]

To that end, we will identify research-based knowledge about the most effective ways to build new families that will be healthy and strong from the beginning, enhance already healthy and strong families, and strengthen families that need to become strong and healthy.

What Is a Strong, Healthy Family?

The term *strong* is used to mean that a couple or family is stable, not at risk of breaking up. It also means that members are not in foster care, incarcerated, or institutionalized. A healthy couple or family is one that is both functional and satisfying to all members. Societal functions of families include these expectations: they produce children, establish legal responsibility for them, and rear them to be healthy, productive members of society. They provide mutual aid to each other, especially in hard times. Emotional support and encouragement are shared along with love and nonsexual affection for each other. There is mutually satisfying sex between adult intimate partners, and sexual behavior is controlled among members to avoid incest, sexual assault, and any sexual violence. Being a member of the strong family means having needs met, including food, clothing, shelter, safety, and a sense of belonging for everyone in the family. The relationship between family members must also be flexible enough to allow the members to interact with systems outside the family to meet needs for mental stimulation (e.g., education), aesthetic interests (e.g., recreational or artistic), or maximizing one's potential (e.g., advancement in the workforce), and spiritual interests.

Which Relationships Should Be Our Focus?

> Dear friends, let us love one another, for love comes
> from God. Everyone who loves has been born of God
> and knows God. Whoever does not love does not know
> God, because God is love (1 John 4:7-8, NIV).

The mark of a Christian in any relationship is love. Therefore, churches are obligated to teach congregants how to demonstrate love toward self, spouse, child, sibling, household members, extended kin, friends, and those persons we meet at church, work, school, or play. There are no exceptions! Wherever there are weak or unhealthy relationships, the lack of Christian love must be understood and explored.

Sometimes the lack of love originates in negative experiences in childhood, adolescence, or adulthood, including experiences with abandonment, abuse, neglect, or exposure to violence. In other instances, it originates in upbringing with antisocial attitudes or values about what is right and wrong. The lack of love, especially toward oneself, is manifested by destructive coping strategies (e.g., abuse or addictions involving food, drugs, alcohol, gambling, sex, or even church involvement). It might show up in an excessive need for power and control over others. In this case, it causes weak and unhealthy relationships in couples, between parents and children, in households, or among extended kin, friends, coworkers, or schoolmates. Our Bible tells us:

> Therefore if there is any consolation in Christ, if any
> comfort of love, if any fellowship of the Spirit, if any
> affection and mercy, fulfill my joy by being like-minded,
> having the same love, being of one accord, of one mind.
> Let nothing be done through selfish ambition or conceit,
> but in lowliness of mind let each esteem others better
> than himself. Let each of you look out not only for his

own interests, but also for the interests of others. (Philippians 2:1-4, NKJV)

Church leaders must teach the patterns of love, humility, and servanthood to boys, girls, men, and women so these patterns can be applied to creating strong, healthy relationships with self and others. It is the acquisition of knowledge, positive attitudes, values, and relationship skills that will provide the climate for healthy marriages and family life. Then selfishness and neediness will cease to block the pathway to loving relationships. Spouses can be flexible enough in their role expectations to allow each other to develop to their highest potential and to live out God's purpose for their lives while leading their children to do likewise.

Strategies and Resources for Ministry

Family-oriented Christian education ministry (CEM) proposes the intentional teaching of males and females of all ages in the knowledge, skills, attitudes, and values necessary for stable, satisfying personal and family life.[12] It includes, of course, biblical education in what it means to live life as a follower of Christ. Teachings on love and justice are pivotal ones for the individual and for interactions within family networks. In addition, age-appropriate lessons are provided on how to get along with others, how to select a spouse, and how to live a satisfying married life, including its sexual aspects. Family-oriented CEM would also include topics such as how to prepare for parenthood and effective parenting skills, including nutrition, meal planning, and family recreation. How to acquire and manage financial and real property as well as how to own a successful business are important topics for the CEM, too.

Jumpin' da Broom: Healthy and Strong from the Beginning

If parents realize that each new baby is designed to grow into adulthood, they may more readily equip children with the very best physical environment to sustain them through life's journey. To this end, CEM instructors should teach fathers and mothers how to be in good health when they conceive a child and where they can receive early prenatal health care. Even before the baby is born, they should enroll in parenting education classes hosted by their church.

As a resource, curriculum materials developed for parents and guardians of black children should be used by well-prepared instructors selected from the congregation. An African American parent training program called *Pulling Together to Rear Our Children—They Grow Up Only Once!* is one such curriculum.[13] Materials, consultation, and instructor training are also available at www.aafle.org. Parents who are equipped to rear children to become happy, healthy, productive members of society, despite its all too often unfairness, will coach their children and advocate on their behalf so they can acquire a good formal education for employment or entrepreneurship. Today and into the future this means not only graduating from high school, but obtaining a vocational, technical, or college degree afterward.

During childhood and adolescence, parents and guardians should be diligent in guiding boys and girls to enjoy all learning—academic, religious, and social—so they can become the best, most well-rounded person possible. Churches can offer classes to parents, adolescents, and young adults, teaching them, as one book title claims, "how to avoid marrying a jerk (or jerkette)"![14]

It is crucial that churches teach both men and women that violence of any kind is incompatible with a strong, healthy relationship, whether in family life or other arenas. Books such as *But I Love Him: Protecting Your Teen Daughter from Controlling, Abusive Dating Relationships*[15] or *Boys into Men: Raising our African American Teenage Sons*[16] are excellent resources for youth ministries. Many churches have created rites of passage programs specifically to prepare young people for the transition from childhood to adulthood. An example of a Christian education ministry to boys provided by the men's ministry and other men of the church is a Baptist Boys-to-Men Program in Indianapolis. According to N. A. Weeden, youth advisor to the group, "We, as a group of men and boys, must go to the streets for outreach ministry as a 'marketing/advertising' effort to 'fish for souls' . . . [to] demonstrate the clear dead end, and oftentimes deadly results, of the street life."[17] He goes on to urge that churches implement rites of passage programs:

> . . . activities in order for the boys to understand and appreciate the goodness of Jesus. . . . Of course, boys being kids, the program needs an element of fun as a springboard to introduce the boys to Jesus via use of creative teaching methods, spontaneous melodramas, interactive games, role-plays, panel discussion, guest speakers, and testimonies.[18]

In a communication to me, Weeden suggested that activities could include "workshops, rap sessions, outdoor activities (e.g., camping, hiking, fishing, horseback riding, and football or basketball games) that most boys and men often enjoy." He suggests that churches should "utilize recreational activities as a 'hook' to get them involved and to provide the opportunity to teach the Bible, academics, black history (e.g., history of blacks in athletics) and the Christian characteristics of real heroes."[19]

To implement these activities, Weeden also suggested that invitations should be made not only to men of the local church but to guests who are:

> [S]incere Christian men, without hidden, self-serving agendas; who "not only talk the talk, but walk the walk," someone to whom the boys can relate. Such men might include professional athletes who have unashamedly professed a hope in Christ and desire to utilize their professional careers for evangelical purposes, or hip hop gurus who have now, after the fact,

committed to reclaiming our youth. Alternatively, news media, iconic celebrities, politicians, public school administrators, and community activists could be invited to bring a meaningful message to the boys in a manner that would bring them to Christ. The goal is to invite someone who can "keep it real" for the glory of God.[20]

Rites of passage programs for girls follow a similar philosophy and format. For an excellent example, see the Atlanta-based Women after God's Own Heart ministry sponsored by the United Methodist Church.[21]

Making Your Good Thing Better!

Following a format similar to that for children, adolescents, and young adults preparing for adult roles, Christian education ministries should be developed for couples as well. The target population should include engaged couples, as well as married couples at every stage of family life (e.g., newlyweds, couples with young children by birth or adoption, couples with adolescents or young adults, or "empty-nesters" who are couples again).[22] A special ministry opportunity exists for couples in the military to secure the stability and quality of their marriages in spite of the demands of worldwide duty.[23] To the same degree as with children and singles, sensitivity to the selection of curriculum material for couples of various ethnic groups is required. *The African American Marriage Enrichment Program: How to Make Your Good Thing Better*[24] is one such tool available to CEM instructors. It is appropriate for couples in which at least one partner is black.

Since some couples are already disillusioned with marriage or family life, and some are in serious jeopardy of violence or divorce, churches should be prepared to provide healing to these relationships. These couples require more attention to healing broken hearts than couples for whom Christian education ministry alone is intended. For those couples whose relationships need more intensive guidance to become healthier and stronger, individual counseling, psychotherapy, life coaching, or couples and family therapy are required. These services should be provided by professionals such as pastoral counselors, social workers, marriage and family therapists, psychologists, psychiatrists, domestic violence practitioners, and substance abuse or addiction recovery specialists. For directories of service providers in these areas, consult resources such as: American Association for Marriage and Family Therapy,[25] National Domestic Violence Hotline,[26] or your state's Healthy Marriage and Family Coalition.[27]

Clergy and lay leaders in the black church are aware of the need for Christian education ministry as well as more intensive, professional services to couples already disillusioned and at their breaking points. However, few churches are equipped to begin the necessary healing ministries to males and females of all ages. This chapter has introduced some of the critical research to describe the scope of the underlying problems and challenges facing the black family as well as evidence of what CEM looks like with practical guides and teaching resources for clergy and laity to develop the resources needed to prepare males and females for marriage. Regardless of the strategy used, a Christian education ministry for the African American congregation and community is imperative. Break the silence and bring to congregants and communities good news, joy, freedom, light, comfort, beauty, gladness, and praise (see Isaiah 61:1-3).

Questions for Those Who Wish to Use the Text as a Teaching Resource[28]

1. How do you define a healthy, loving, committed marriage?

2. How do you define a healthy family?

3. What signs might indicate that church attendees who are presently in healthy, loving, and committed marriages have become silent?

■ Do they maintain a neutral attitude concerning the benefits they enjoy in their marriages?

■ Do they feel the need not to offend those living other lifestyles?

■ Do they avoid bringing attention to the disparities they live beside in their church communities?

4. How is the church organized to develop lay ministries to families?

■ Does it utilize the skills of professionally trained individuals among its congregants?

■ Is there a place for the sensitive development of mentoring married couples to influence and support the educational efforts of the church in ministry to families?

5. How can the pastor become the principal model of healthy marriage and family relationships?

■ Is the pastor the spiritual voice of the community concerning healthy marriage and family relationships?

■ Is the pastor committed to developing healthy marriage and family relationships in the congregation by leadership and lifestyle?

■ Is the pastor committed to developing healthy marriage and family relationships in the community?

6. What mechanisms are in place for the church to train clergy and lay leaders to provide Christian education ministry to couples and families? Where can you get the training you need to get started?[29]

NOTES

1. http://www.cdc.gov/nchs/data/hus/hus06.pdf#003. Accessed April 19, 2007.

2. *Breaking the Silence for the Good of All People*, program booklet. National Council of Churches, 2006. See http://www.ncc-cusa.org/pdfs/btsprogram.pdf. Accessed April 19, 2007.

3. See http://www.hhs.gov/news/press/2002pres/welfare.html for more information about the Personal Responsibility and

Work Opportunity Reconciliation Act of 1996 (PRWORA). Accessed April 19, 2007.

4. See http://www.cdc.gov/nchs/data/nvsr/nvsr54/nvsr54_20.pdf. Accessed April 19, 2007.

5. Richard M. Lerner, *Liberty: Thriving Civic Engagement among America's Youth* (Thousand Oaks, CA: The Sage Program on Applied Developmental Science, 2004).

6. See http://www.cdc.gov/mmwr/preview/mmwrhtml/rr5022 a1.htm. Accessed April 19, 2007.

7. See http://www.cdc.gov/nchs/data/nvsr/nvsr54/nvsr54_02.pdf. Accessed April 19, 2007.

8. See http://www.cdc.gov/nchs/data/hus/hus05.pdf#052. Accessed April 19, 2007.

9. See http://www.cdc.gov/hiv/resources/factsheets/PDF/msm.pdf. Accessed April 19, 2007.

10. Phillip Zimbardo, *Psychology and Life,* 12th ed. (Glenview, IL: Scott, Foresman and Co., 1988), 101.

11. See http://www.lightplanet.com/mormons/daily/fhe/strong/chastity.htm.

12. See James C. Perkins, *Building Up Zion's Walls,* ed. Jean Alicia Elster (Valley Forge, PA: Judson, 1999). For family life education content areas across the lifespan, see the PowerPoint presentation available at http://www.ncfr.org/cfle/FLE_prod ucts.htm.

13. Lorraine C. Blackman, *Pulling Together to Rear Our Children—They Grow Up Only Once! Instructor's Manual* (Indiana University School of Social Work, 2005). See http://www.aafle.org.

14. John Van Epp, *How to Avoid Marrying a Jerk: The Foolproof Way to Follow Your Heart without Losing Your Mind* (New York: McGraw-Hill, 2006). See http://www.no jerks.com.

15. Jill Murray, *But I Love Him: Protecting Your Teen Daughter from Controlling, Abusive Dating Relationships.* (New York: HarperCollins, 2000).

16. Nancy Boyd-Franklin, A. J. Franklin, and Pamela A. Toussaint, *Boys into Men: Raising our African American Teenage Sons* (New York: Dutton Adult Books, 2001).

17. N. A. Weeden, "Things Ain't What They Used to Be—But They Can Be with God's Grace." Unpublished paper (Indianapolis: Simmons College of Kentucky, Indianapolis Extension, 2006), 5.

18. Ibid., 6.

19. Weeden, personal communication with author.

20. Ibid.

21. See http://www.wagohmin.org.

22. For models of premarital and marriage education programs, see www.smartmarriages.com or http://www.healthy marriageinfo.org/marriageedu.

23. See http://www.defenselink.mil/news/Jan2006/20060127_4034.htm.

24. Blackman, *Pulling Together*.

25. See www.aafle.org for curriculum materials, consultation, and instructor training.

26. See www.therapistlocator.net/therapistlocator/index.asp or www.ndvh.org/help/help_in_area.html.

27. See: http://www.smartmarriages.com/directory_browse.html#STATES.

28. Gratitude goes to Seventh-day Adventist pastor Willie Lee of Houston, Texas, and AME senior steward Virginia Cooper of Nashville, Tennessee, for framing the reflection questions.

29. For numerous articles on marriage education or healthy relationships, log on to http://www.govmine.com and search keywords "marriage education" or "healthy relationships."

CHAPTER 4

Exploring the Meaning and Possibilities of Black Fatherhood Today

EDWARD P. WIMBERLY, PhD, RUEBEN WARREN, DDS, AND ANNE STREATY WIMBERLY, PhD

The Meaning of Fatherhood

We define *fatherhood* as the function of caring for and nurturing the next generation of offspring from birth to young adulthood. As a function, fatherhood is biologically specific in that it involves the male gender, but it is not synonymous with biologically providing the sperm that impregnates the egg. More precisely, fatherhood is more than impregnating. It is *generative* and *relational* in nature. It is *generative* because it facilitates the growth of a child from birth to young adulthood, and it is *relational* because it requires regular interaction between the child and the father. In other words, fatherhood can involve any male who fulfills the caring and nurturing task on a regular basis over a significant period of time.

Fatherhood not only transcends the biological impregnating act, but it is also an *outgrowth of community*. Fatherhood is rooted and grounded in a community consisting of couples, family and extended family members, relatives, and small social networks of people sometimes referred to as a village. The village is made up of blood relatives as well as people who become members of the village because of their regular interaction and activity within the community over a significant period of time. Within this communal context, fathering is an outgrowth of the village's efforts to provide relational ties that sustain the child through the many transitions from birth to young adulthood. It is the community that sanctions the father to act on its behalf to care for and nurture the child from birth to young adulthood, and the community provides other parent surrogates to assist in this fathering function.

As indicated, the fathering function takes place *throughout the life cycle* of the child from birth to young adulthood. The life cycle consists of infancy to early childhood (under 1 year old), early childhood to middle childhood (ages 1–4), from middle childhood to adolescence (ages 5–14), and adolescence to young adulthood (ages 15–24). Each one of these stages has certain challenges and tasks for the child to accomplish, and it is the father, along with the other members of the village, who assist the child in transitioning through these stages. Without this assistance the child can get stuck in a particular stage and cannot proceed to the next stage of development.

Fathering is communally connected as well, because the father draws from the communal wisdom that provides tried and true methods of parenting that are transmitted from one generation to the next. In this sense of transmitting values, fathering by its very nature must be cross-generational. More precisely, fathering involves at least three, if not more, generations, and fathering becomes impoverished without such cross-generational relationships. Thus, fathering is assisted by parents, grandparents, great-grandparents, relatives, the neighborhood, and the village. The role of these people is to keep alive the parenting wisdom that has developed over the years along with new discoveries that come as a result of the behavioral sciences.

Finally, fatherhood requires maturity of the male who performs the father function. *Maturity* here refers to the confidence and capacity to take full responsibility for one's own life and choices rooted and grounded in how well the father has negotiated his own developmental tasks from birth to young adulthood. Thus, the capacity for fatherhood is developmental. In addition, maturity also involves the capacity to be *significantly connected* with members of the village, and especially with the three-generation family. Disconnected males have very little capacity for empathy, which is required for caring and nurturing. Moreover, disconnected males also suffer from being stuck in earlier stages of childhood development. In short, maturity requires the capacity for personal agency where one can act responsibly as well as the capacity for connecting with others across generations.

By way of summary, fatherhood is more than the biological act of impregnating. It is both generative and relational. It is grounded in communal networks, and it transmits communal wisdom to children as they negotiate the life transitions from birth to young adulthood. Fatherhood also requires personal maturity as well as the capacity for being connected significantly.

Such a definition of fatherhood grows out of many years of research on the black family from slavery to the present time. Communal parenting practices along with cross-generational relationships have been the strength of African American family life over the years.[1] In addition, the communal understanding of fatherhood relates to spiritual resources that came from black religion and African spirituality. The black church was part of the communal networks mentioned, and it was black church spirituality that was appealed to when there were attempts to reconstruct black families after the abolition of slavery.[2] One basic value of this definition of fatherhood is that it provides a framework for identifying best practices for enabling black men to become fathers in the relational and generative sense.

A Life-Cycle Perspective on African American Fatherhood

A life-cycle perspective on fatherhood presupposes that parents have achieved some success in resolving the major developmental transitions that led them to adulthood. Thus, parenthood assumes that both the mother and father have adequately resolved those age-appropriate transitions from childhood to adolescence, from adolescence to young adulthood, and from young adulthood to adulthood.

Childhood takes place from the time of the birth of a child up until he or she approaches adolescence. For our purposes, childhood is composed of three stages: age 0–1, ages 1–4 years, and ages 5–14 years. During childhood there are certain emotional, interpersonal, and social tasks that must be accomplished and that are tied closely to a child's biological makeup and his or her maturational genetic print. Moreover, the emotional and interpersonal environment in the home; the quality of the relationships between the father and mother and other family members; the father's involvement with the child and whether he is in the home or not; the quality of parenting; family dynamics; and external factors outside the home, such as employment; level of education of the parents; and racism and racial discrimination all impact that child directly and through family members. The following factors also impact the child's life cycle.

From 0–1 years of age, the primary developmental task of the child is to establish trust with one's primary caregivers as well as with one's relational environment. Trust is the foundation of the child's inner world, and relationships with significant others are vital. The child's trust develops from the quality of relationships with his or her primary caregivers, and the child is completely dependent upon positive relationships for laying the foundation for future self-esteem.[3] Because of this, parents cannot afford to be preoccupied with factors that will negatively impact the relational environment on which the child depends. Parents must be free of concerns about economic survival, social discrimination, job-related controversy, and other factors. In other words, a good-enough, conflict-free environment will foster trust in the child.

Such a conflict-free environment is also essential when the child transitions into the ages 1–4 developmental cycle. During this time period the child internalizes the attitudes of significant others, and these internalizations become the cornerstones for building the sense of self. Another related task during this childhood phase is for the child to learn to control his or her bodily functions without the primary caregivers being overly controlling or overly permissive. Too much control or, conversely, lack of control, leads to personality conflicts that undermine the child's emotional development. Consequently, the ability of the significant others to respond to the child's age-appropriate tasks is critical for the child's development.

When the child moves to the 5–14 age range, there will be age-appropriate tasks that the child must accomplish to enter into the school setting. Among those tasks is initiation of exploration of the new environment. There the child must develop social and interpersonal skills with peers, learn to manipulate his or her environment, and develop a host of skills that will serve the child in taking full responsibility in life as an adult. The primary caregivers must be emotionally equipped, relatively conflict-free, and not preoccupied with economic survival and unresolved developmental tasks so that they can be present with their child or children as they undertake these tasks.

Adolescence includes ages 15–24 and is characterized by an attempt to achieve personal identity. Personal identity is the major task of adolescent formation and includes an individual's accumulated sense of self that has developed since birth along with the culture's confirmation of that accrued self through the offering of a concrete vocation through which to express it.[4] In addition, there is a grave danger of being recruited into negative identities due to negative images as portrayed in music by rap artists, by intentionally poor education, and through police profiling of black youth.[5]

The end result of a negative identity is the failure to establish a positive identity that is essential for developing a life structure. A life structure is an overarching structure formed as a result of the choices one makes about marriage, parenting, occupation, key friendships, and relationships to parents and relatives. It forms a bridge between the inner self and the outside social world.[6] In young adulthood this structure is formed by learning to be an adult by making such choices as occupation, marriage, and parenting. The ability to form a life structure results in developing a dream for one's life, in obtaining mentoring relationships for entering occupations, and in building solid marital and family relationships. The dream is all about becoming one's future self with a sense of movement in positive directions.

It is clear that the external social world of African American adolescents and young adult males impacts their life structure and identity. The absense of an "external network of institutions that provide roles for each person's engagement is clearly detrimental to development," according to Winston Gooden.[7] He goes on to say that African American men must engage in social and cultural roles that are valued by community, and without such engagement, one's personal sense of significance and development is stunted and life's meaning is thwarted.[8]

Significant in young adulthood is the reality that the capacity for intimacy is one of the best predictors of a maturing person, for marital success, for the ability to parent, and for occupational success in adulthood and midlife.[9] African American adolescents and young adults value marriage and long-term relationships, but it is difficult to maintain long-term relationships without achieving the valued and sanctioned social roles. To compensate for failures from the appropriate life structure to a meaningful life, some African American males turn to a distorted view of manhood to build self-esteem.[10]

African American men carry their life structure into adulthood. Adulthood has three stages. The period between 25–44 is characterized by the individual needing to accomplish certain age-appropriate tasks that began in the earlier stages. This includes knowing who one is apart from others, taking full responsibility for one's own life, and making choices that set the directions for one's life and life structure for the next nineteen years, as well as choices about marriage and family, vocation, and religious involvement.

Ages 45–64 mark the period of transition from adulthood into middle adulthood, and this transition is marked by the need to alter one's life structure in light of the physical decline of the body, the change from a youthful orientation toward the beginning of a new orientation for living the last half of one's life, the need to think about goals one will never realize, and the need to build one's life structure on a more secure spiritual basis. The major tasks are to build a life structure that informs how one is to leave a legacy for the next generation and how one is to make one's life count. During this later phase of life, one needs to be sure to take advantage of the time that remains. Finally, age 65 marks retirement for most people. This is supposed to be the phase of becoming an elder in the community and being the custodian of the wisdom that has developed over the years. It is a stage for preparing for one's inevitable death, and one's life structure needs to be altered considerably.

Developmental theory suggests that successful resolving of developmental tasks in the previous stages will eventually produce positive adaptation and adjustment in later life stages. Problems begin, however, when previous unresolved developmental tasks resurface and need to be resolved in the later life stages, because the unresolved problems of previous stages do not disappear. Thus, the factors that cause problems in resolving developmental tasks in particular life stages need to be identified. The impact that they have on life stages needs to be spelled out as well.

Understanding the External Factors That Affect Fatherhood

Three external factors influence all developmental life transitions. They influence how parents interact with their children, and they influence how adults go through their adult life cycle stages. These factors are challenges throughout the life cycle for African Americans from birth to death and include bicultural challenges, the loss of cross-generational connections, and the culture of poverty.

Bicultural challenges refer to living in two cultures at one time with one culture holding out goals for achievement while preventing certain groups from accessing the means of achieving these goals. Preventing the achieving of certain goals takes place through the denial of access to adequate education, employment, and racial discrimination resulting in the second culture, which is called the culture of poverty. Thus, African Americans must learn to live in a world where they are criticized for not achieving their aspirations, while at the same time being denied access to the means for achieving these goals. Impoverished African Americans find themselves in a double bind, and this double bind is called living biculturally or living in two cultures at once.

The culture of poverty is the result of having access denied to achieving the goals of society. The culture of poverty refers to learned attitudinal and behavioral responses to the lack of educational and employment opportunities for achieving access to the goals held out by the wider culture. It is learning to live attitudinally and behaviorally toward a hostile environment where one is denied access to the skills necessary to escape poverty. The attitudes and behaviors become convictions and beliefs about the self, others, and one's place in life, as well as one's expectations for life. Such beliefs in the culture of poverty contributes to the attitudes of hopelessness and loss of self-esteem resulting in multiproblem families, anger, rage, purposelessness, and a sense of impotence.[11]

The culture of poverty and living biculturally are compounded by the loss of cross-generational connections. The support that people need to transcend the conditions in which they live takes the efforts of an entire village. Disconnections and loss of cross-generational connections as the result of the advances in technology and lack of sanctioned support for nurturing and caring values across generations by the wider culture are devastating to African Americans in the culture of poverty.

All three of these factors impact the way life tasks are accomplished in each adult. For example, culture poverty causes the life-cycle stages to be arrested and truncated. Households often become female-headed rather than dual-headed. Invariably numerous and unpredictable life crises occur and bring instability. Many impediments to accomplishing age-appropriate tasks arise. Individuals and families are overwhelmed by stress, and family resources are depleted. Individuals, especially fathers, fall behind on the accomplishing of age-appropriate life-cycle tasks, and are prevented from advancing to the next stage. Thus, many African American fathers in the culture of poverty have difficulty taking on parenting tasks because of poor education, lack of adequate employment, and loss of hope. Being cut off from relational connections makes it more difficult to access the skills needed to accomplish age-appropriate developmental tasks.

The Church's Response
While it is not too late to intervene in the lives of adults, middle adults, and older adults in handling the culture of poverty, it is much better to begin at the optimal, promotional, primary, and secondary stages during birth to young adulthood. Using public policy to address unequal access to education and employment, working to restore the connections across generations, helping people thrive despite the obstacles, and helping them find resources for hope and self-esteem in the earlier stages of the life cycle is very important. A key element is to secure the life structure in such a way that African American males are sustained and encouraged as they seek to engage cultural roles that are valued and respected. This element promotes a positive sense of self.

Promoting Community Health by Attending to Black Fatherhood
First, let's look at the public health model. This model, as proposed here, follows four approaches. They include the following:

■ promoting health
■ primary prevention
■ secondary prevention
■ tertiary prevention

Promoting health seeks to foster optimal health of the community by securing, maintaining, preserving, and promoting the relational ties of the village, social networks, neighborhood, cross-generational bonds, strong mediating structures (marriage, family, extended family, churches, and fraternal organizations), communally based healing practices, and oral traditions that promote fatherhood of African American men. The practices that promote health include public policy efforts to promote relational ties through valuing the role of care and nurture that must support parenting in our culture.

Primary prevention protects the relational networks through promoting social policies, consultation and education with governmental institutions, social agencies, the urban planning entity, and community groups that impact the lives of fathers. Primary prevention also assures employment opportunities as well as educational opportunities for African American fathers to take advantage of thriving economic times. The practices that promote primary prevention include ensuring the ability of community networks to continue to function well.

Secondary prevention requires early intervention when any network of relationships that support African American fatherhood begins to collapse. The practices of secondary prevention intervene in families and social networks to find early cases or problems.

Tertiary prevention fosters major rehabilitation of those fathers who have become disconnected. The practices of tertiary prevention must prepare these fathers to reenter their families and the community.

Activities necessary for accomplishing these preventions are listed below, but first we must point out four major assumptions when promoting the health of the community by attending to fatherhood:

1. A holistic approach to public health requires interdependent family relationships. We must take into consideration the roles and responsibilities of parents, children, grandmothers and grandfathers, aunts and uncles, and any others who have no biological or genetic connection yet are nonetheless family.

2. Holistic public health efforts require integration of individuals in mainstream society. Black men are increasingly becoming relational refugees who are disconnected from mainstream society.[12] Such disconnection results in early school dropout rates, legal problems, high incarceration rates and criminal activity, joblessness/unemployment, substance abuse and addiction, violence of all kinds, absent parents, poor performance in schools, the breakdown of families at the core, and the absence of life skills.

3. The major task of the church and community is to help black men and fathers reconnect with the relational ties of the community and increase their involvement in their families and the raising of their children.

4. One of the basic intervention methods for connecting African American men with their children and building communal ties is the use of the cultural tendency to employ narrative oral skills.

To undertake the promotions as described by the public health model, certain activities are necessary. They include:

1. Promoting Health

■ Address public policy to assure the quality of relational connecting in marriages, families, extended families, neighborhood, cross generational (at least three generations) and strong mediating structures, including institutions standing between individuals and wider social institutions, such as schools, neighborhood organizations, boys and girls clubs, recreation centers, and churches

■ Provide support through regular policy and consistent involvement of fathers across at least three generations

■ Ensure and support the establishment, and continue voluntary groups and community agencies

■ Support relational values of caring and nurturing as essential for fostering responsible parenting through public media

■ Ensure that government, school systems, and social agencies address employment and educational opportunities in specific communities

■ Identify and support community revitalization projects through involvement in community-based organizations, community development corporations, partnerships with government organizations, civic and church groups, charter schools, and others

■ Support efforts to address character development in schools and social agencies

2. Primary Prevention

■ Provide consultation and education to schools, government organizations, community agencies, churches, civic groups, urban planning and development organizations, community revitalization groups, and others that address policies supporting relational values of caring and nurturing

■ Ensure that the community provides jobs, job training, and the institutionalization of programs and policies that support fatherhood

■ Ensure public transportation to jobs and education

3. Secondary Prevention

■ Use consultation and education as tools of early intervention for marriages, families, communal support systems, and community groups that have contact with fathers who have children. This consultation and education will focus on employment opportunities and job skills; appropriate educational preparation; the life cycles of children, youth, and young adults; and parenting and coparenting skills. It should also provide forums for discussions and learning about masculinity and fatherhood as well as strengthen fathers' relational skills, marital and family life cycles and related tasks for couples and families at each stage

■ Work with mentors to perform surrogate fathering roles with children, adolescents, and young adults

■ Implement character and life-skill development through educational and mentoring programs
■ Support the connection between personal agency (achieving developmental growth) and its connection to political efficacy (helping others to address concerns to improve our communities)

4. Tertiary Prevention
■ Provide opportunities to work with agencies that work with fathers who have disconnected from significant and support relationships
■ Provide psychological counseling and addiction recovery counseling
■ Provide job skills education
■ Provide training in anger management and nonviolent conflict management in relationships with spouses and children
■ Provide education about the meaning of manhood and fatherhood
■ Provide a context for exploration of family of origin issues surrounding parenting and being male
■ Work with courts and prerelease programs to ensure better adjustment to society after incarceration

Participants

When it comes to promoting health and initiating primary prevention, participants should include those who prepare and frame public policies impacting values and communal/relational ties, job policies, educational opportunities, and community development. These individuals include people working in the schools, neighborhood organizations, urban planning organizations, community revitalization groups, media, and local government agencies that foster relational ties.

In the area of secondary prevention, the audience includes married couples, families, and extended families as well as community mediating structures and support systems in which fathers and boys of all ages (child, adolescent, and young adult) are present.

Participants in tertiary prevention should encompass disconnected fathers and the agencies that seek to rehabilitate men and prepare them to return to community and productive lives.

Outcomes

The proposed outcomes of the public health policy include several important dimensions to promoting healthy relationships and strengthening the black family and community. Generally speaking, these outcomes may be grouped under the dimensions of awareness, education, and implementation.

Awareness

■ Increased awareness of relational values of care and nurturing and how they are essential sanctions for parenting
■ Broad recognition of the significance of father involvement
■ Increased creation and awareness of job opportunities
■ Heightened awareness of individual, marital, and family life cycles and related tasks
■ Learning-awareness programs for addressing rehabilitation concerns
■ Heightened awareness of the causes and effects of disconnection, including substance abuse, violence, chronic unemployment, ab-sentee fathers, inadequate education, poor job skills, criminal activity, and distorted understandings of manhood and fatherhood

Education

■ General education in character formation, self-esteem, and life skills
■ Refined education about masculinity and the meanings and roles of fatherhood—and revised behavior based on those changed definitions and understandings
■ Education concerning the value of father involvement in family life
■ Increased education and implementation of coparenting and parenting skills

■ Education and training in the acquisition and expansion of job skills

Implementation
■ Improved behavior in healthy fathering and greater support to parents who are serious about raising their children
■ Implementation and support of policies that strengthen relational ties
■ Establishment of community agencies and groups that support marriages, families, and mediating structures
■ Institutionalization of caring and nurturing values at the community level
■ Broad exercise of employment and educational opportunities
■ Improved relationships with children based on life-cycle stages and tasks
■ Adequate economic resources for families
■ Improved community health through strong relational and nurturing institutions

The public health policy program is unquestionably ambitious. But considering the daunting challenges of the African American community, it must be. We must move beyond insight to concerted efforts toward connection and involvement in relationships and fathering. The program outlined here is not meant simply to uncover or break the silence concerning the complexities of fatherhood in today's context. The program also seeks to elevate the importance of fatherhood in the overall health of family life. Together we can change the disturbing trends affecting the black family by persistent action and reasonable policy changes at the local, state, and national levels.

NOTES
1. Edward P. Wimberly, *Counseling African American Marriages and Families* (Louisville: Westminster John Knox, 1997), 7–10.

2. Ibid., 32–37.

3. Erik H. Erikson, *Insight and Responsibility* (New York: Norton, 1964).

4. Erik H. Erikson, *Identity: Youth and Crisis* (New York: Norton, 1968).

5. Edward P. Wimberly, *Relational Refugees: Alienation and Reincorporation in African American Churches and Communities* (Nashville: Abingdon, 2006); Wimberly, *African American Pastoral Care and Counseling: The Politics of Oppression and Empowerment* (Cleveland, OH: Pilgrim, 2006).

6. Winston Gooden, *Development of Black Men in Early Adulthood* (Berkeley, CA: Cobb & Henry, 1989).

7. Ibid., 84.

8. Ibid., 85.

9. Ibid., 85.

10. Ibid., 86–87.

11. Edward P. Wimberly, 1997, 55–56; Anne Streaty Wimberly, *Honoring African American Elders: A Ministry in the Soul Community* (San Francisco: Jossey-Bass, 1997).

12. Ronald Mincy, *Black Males Left Behind* (Washington, DC: Urban Institute Press, 2006). Cited in Erik Eckholm's "Plight Deepens for Black Men, Studies Warn," *The New York Times,* March 20, 2006.

CHAPTER 5

Black Men, the Church, and Family in Hip-Hop Culture

JOHNNY B. HILL, PhD

Fathers, do not provoke your children to anger, but bring
them up in the discipline and instruction of the Lord.
(Ephesians 6:4, NRSV)

Of my father I know nothing. Slavery had no recognition
of fathers, as none of families.
—Frederick Douglass

In light of the fact that most African American households are led
by women, there is an even more urgent call to address the issue
of fatherhood in particular and black men in the church in general. Because of racism and cultural stereotypes and perceptions,
very little attention is given to fatherhood within and outside the
commodious pews of churches. At the same time, research indicates that when fathers develop close relationships with their children, there is an increased likelihood that marriages will remain
intact, and the economic, emotional, psychological, and physical
well-being of black families will be on more stable footing.

Popular culture is bombarded with images of the absent father and deadbeat dad. These images are far more damaging when it comes to black men, images that seep into the subconscious of the black male experience beginning as early as preadolescent years. I agree with Jennifer Hamer when she observes, "Popular perceptions of African American men historically have represented extremes."[1] Those extremes range from pernicious notions of the hypersexual to the emasculated, dangerous, intellectually inferior, comical, or lazy male. Black men are constantly battling the forces contributing to low expectations and capacities for fatherhood and family life. The critical question however, is what it means to be a black father in today's social climate. How do we begin to understand the challenges of a vast number of black youth whose fathers live outside the home? There are certain particular social problems that disproportionately impact African American males in their quest to perform the duties of fatherhood. This chapter offers a critical appraisal of the spiritual and social forces at work in the life of black fathers and shows how those forces affect the entire family.

Social, Political, and Economic Context of Black Fathers

Any discussion regarding the role of the church in supporting black fatherhood must begin by thinking about the historical and contemporary experience of black men and the church. Since the inception of the black church in America, African American men have played an active role in its leadership and overall ministry. Richard Allen and Absalom Jones first led a mass exodus to establish African American congregations throughout the nation in the nineteenth century. The presence of African American men in the black church was perhaps at its height during the civil rights movement when African American men, through the voices of leaders like Martin Luther King Jr., found dignity, respect, and affirmation.

In a post–civil rights era, however, the African American male presence in black churches has come to reflect startling trends in wider society. The problem of joblessness, urban decay, and dilapidated educational systems, encouraged by the development of a bourgeoisie church has contributed to increased absence of the black male presence. Unfortunately, the media has fed the public news about black men either on their way to prison, serving in prison or jail, or newly released from prison. Popular columnist and scholar Earl Ofari Hutchinson writes, "The image of young blacks prone on the ground, handcuffed against walls and over the hoods of police cars make better copy anyway."[2] Negative images overwhelm our culture about the nature of this problem. Is there really a crisis? While the idea of "crisis" implies a temporary deviation from a more suitable norm or that a more secured condition preceded the current state, for black males evidence suggests that the present situation is not at all temporary; in fact, the severity of the problem is increasing.

More than one million black men are in prison or jail or on parole. That's a million fathers, sons, grandsons, brothers, and uncles locked up and locked down—mostly the result of a lack of decent jobs in the urban centers since factories shut down in the early seventies and manufacturing shifted toward globalization. In a visit to Cook County Jail in Chicago, Illinois, I observed firsthand the severity of the problem. The facility was inundated with hundreds of strong black men devoid of dignity and longing for freedom and fulfillment. William Julius Wilson, the acclaimed sociologist, has brought the point home in his books *When Work Disappears* and *The Declining Significance of Race*.[3] He observes how an almost permanent underclass is developing in the urban settings of America. These are the people who have been essentially locked out from the mainstream marketplace. Because of globalization and technology, jobs and cheap labor are now outsourced overseas permanently. By addressing the many dynamics of the black male experience, in a broad sense, the church is better poised to strengthen the relationships between black fathers, and their families.

John Hurst Adams, as one of the contributors to Gayraud Wilmore's *Black Men in Prison*, responds very poignantly to the question, "Where do we go from here?"[4] Proposing that there must be an "innovative mission and ministry" to confront the issue, Adams outlines key strategies that focus on: (1) theology and policy, (2) education and educational materials, (3) advocacy and strategy, (4) ministry and programs, and (5) monitoring and networking.[5] The theology is the basis upon which we define the moral, humane, and political definitions of the issue at hand. It is these theological positions that empower and motivate people to act and ultimately revise policy. It is important to formulate and conceptualize a theology that is consistent with the gospel of Jesus Christ that offers a spirit of liberation to those who seek to engage this ministry. We must develop a "theology of the judicial and penal systems," says Adams.[6]

Educational work and educational materials go hand in hand as we must not depend on political or social structures to educate, inform, and teach our people. For example, through means of education, church leaders may be sensitized to the urgency of black male youth imprisonment and place this at the highest priority in their program agendas and budgets. Advocacy and strategy means organizing and even protesting in explicit ways to increase the consciousness of this problem and what it means to the future of the black community. The other method of response the church has available is a number of tried and true ministry programs (e.g., pen pals, visitations, halfway houses, reentry support and training programs, job placement, family, church, and community support systems). Lastly, Adams posits that we must monitor what is happening in this area on a continual basis and develop networks to stay abreast of systemic problems that need to be exposed, investigated, and understood.[7]

Andrew Billingsley's *Mighty Like a River: The Black Church and Social Reform*, specifies other ways black churches have sought to deal with the current situation facing black male imprisonment.[8] Billingsley highlights the creative strategies of black churches to work with the educational system, become central in the lives of challenged youths, and create new educational structures for youth development. One example is that of Jenkins High School, where a group of black youths were involved in a fight on school grounds. Two of the young men over 16 years old were sentenced by penal authorities to thirty days in jail, which would result in their being retained in their present grade for another year. Through the intervention of Rev. Thurmond Tillman (pastor of First African Baptist Church), the "troubled youth" were able to maintain their progress as students and be fruitful to the entire student body by performing community service and speaking out against violence.

Another example is St. Paul's Academy, formed under the leadership of Rev. Henry Delaney and the St. Paul C.M.E. Church. The uniqueness of this institution is that it was founded exclusively for black boys. Contrary to what many felt would be a disaster, the program has wrought enormous success.[9]

Billingsley also presents the Urban Christian Academy, which has worked closely with an academic school to encourage young boys in discipline, strong academics, and leadership. For the church to move beyond its walls to confront the issue of youth imprisonment is highly consistent with the historical and theological tradition of the black church as rooted in a prophetic spirit of social reform. Billingsley contends, "This movement of the black church's influence from the crises of the civil rights era to the contemporary crisis among black male youths attests to the resilience and adaptability of this institution," and it thus attests to the reform spirit ignited long ago.[10]

There is a visible presence of African American men in leadership roles in the black church who serve as deacons, trustees, clergy, and to some extent, in auxiliary ministries. On the other hand, the presence of African American men in the pews of black churches is relatively minimal. In most mainline churches, there is a growing sense that the church is irrelevant to the needs and concerns of African American men, and thus unnecessary. Additionally, the mounting apolitical stance and emotionalism in churches is often viewed as uncritical and detached from the concrete realities affecting the African American male experience.

The African American male experience in America has been characterized by humiliation, domination, and exploitation. Historically, the church was the powerful space in which the black male could experience what Howard Thurman called "somebodyness." It was the church that provided affirmation of human dignity and self-worth. By affirming that the African American man was created in the image of God, the church also was a significant force for empowering black men to fight for social change, become entrepreneurs, educators, politicians, and spiritual leaders. If the church is to regain a strong presence of African American men and develop strong fathers, it must seek to address the spiritual and material needs of this experience within and beyond the pews of the church.

Challenges in the Church

In many churches there is a lack of understanding and appreciation for the generational forces at work regarding black fathers. Often the cultural perceptions about black males being prone to violence obscure the possibilities for meaningful efforts to support black fatherhood. Part of combating this perception involves confronting the stereotype of the absent father, which contributes to the low priority given to the role of fathers in shaping the life and destiny of children. One of the greatest challenges in churches is confronting traditional norms and practices that marginalize black males from meaningful involvement in church life. It is very common that compartmentalization in churches—fragmentation of programs, events, activities, and ministries—leads to a lack of intentionality in the area of men's ministries in general, fatherhood in particular.

Confronting the obstacles related to black fatherhood is multi-dimensional. It requires awareness and advocacy, both in the church and in the community. Both must address policy issues related to education, incarceration, joblessness, homelessness, and father's rights, as well as holding fathers accountable. In the book of Genesis, we read that where Abram went, "Lot went with him" (12:4; cf.13:1, 5, NIV). There must be more emphasis on becoming mentors both within and outside the church walls. At the same time, churches must dismiss "either/or" language and embrace partnership and communal responsibility. Space needs to be available to affirm and celebrate mothers and mentors, while seeking to enhance father involvement.

Establishing resource centers and partnerships in churches and communities specifically designed to support black fathers is simply one way of approaching the various dimensions of black fatherhood. By forming meaningful partnerships with existing organizations (e.g., Boy's Club, YMCA, Boy Scouts/Girl Scouts, Departments of Family and Youth Services, private youth agencies, etc.) churches and groups can maximize their resources while meeting the needs of a larger constituency. Another very important consideration is to move toward more "holistic" strategies when approaching men's and father's ministries. For example, ministry to fathers and husbands should not be viewed as separate from ministry to youth and children. By thinking differently and creatively about nurturing black fathers in the life of the church, churches will move more steadily and faithfully in an effort to meet the needs of the black family amid current social realities.

Black Fatherhood in Today's Culture

Reflecting on black fatherhood today demands that close attention be given to the social, cultural, and economic trends impacting the overall black male experience. This is particularly true for black male youth. I would argue that fatherhood does not simply begin with the biological relationship after the birth of a child. Fatherhood begins with the formation and development of black male youth as they begin to envision their role as fathers in adulthood. It is extremely difficult to reflect qualities of a committed and loving father in the absence of intentional and close models of fatherhood. For that reason, this chapter is especially devoted to understanding the experience of black male youth and ways in which the church can help form them into committed and loving fathers.

One of the trends that has shaped black fatherhood is hip-hop culture. Hip-hop is a cultural phenomenon that emerged in the early 1980s primarily in urban settings and is characterized by rejection of established social norms, revolt against preestablished rules of behavior, and disdain for the "institutional church." The recent Hollywood movie *Get Rich or Die Tryin'*, starring the popular rapper 50 Cent, depicts a young man born in the ghetto, abandoned by his father, and surrounded by severe poverty. Entangled in the fast world of urban drug culture, the character 50 Cent portrays desires to escape his impending doom and, in the process, save his son. The movie gives enormous insight into the fact that most young black fathers, regardless of their existential circumstances, do want to be strong, caring, and supportive fathers. Subsequently, the church is given the unique opportunity and obligation to develop creative strategies and methods of supporting, affirming, and empowering black fathers for the sake of the overall health of the family unit.

Fatherhood and Black Male Youth Development

Perhaps the most powerful strategy that could be adopted to develop strong fathers is to be intentional about black male youth development. When fathers and mentors model and show young males what it means to be a father, there is a greater likelihood that future generations will reap the harvest of what a strong father brings to the family unit. Afrocentric thinkers have responded to the issue of black males by pointing to their social, cultural, and psychological development. Ronald Mincy, in his *Nurturing Young Black Males*, focuses highly on the developmental needs of young black males yet lacks the Afrocentric perspective to a large extent. Those who have advocated Afrocentric approaches have placed a considerable amount of weight on rites-of-passage programs. Paul Hill Jr., an Afrocentrist, maintains that "the process of African Americans creating our own reality and taking control of the socialization of our youth involves Rites-of-Passage that are African-centered."[11] In other words, the full weight and measure of the African historical and cultural legacy is the prism by which youth develop a sense of identity, perspective, and place in history and from which society is shaped and molded. Through an African-centered rite of passage, a new way of thinking and developing emerges that is informed by African roots and traditions.

Hill clearly states that rites-of-passage exist as a strategy for life-cycle development and not as a panacea for resurrection of the masses. Other programs that have proven to be effective should not be abandoned but rather enhanced through African-centered rites-of-passage programs. For instance, the Boy Scouts of America, instead of being replaced, could incorporate a rites-of-passage merit badge for black troops. In order for rites-of-passage programs to be more effective, however, Hill suggests the institutionalization of such programs.[12] Regrettably, this has been met with opposition by major black social institutions such as churches and mosques because it is perceived as contrary to their belief systems. Amid resistance, some black church leaders are implementing "Christocentric" rites-of-passage programs nevertheless—leaders including Rev. Frank Fair of Norristown, Pennsylvania, Rev. Wendell Anthony of Detroit, Rev. Dr. Jeremiah A. Wright Jr. of Chicago, and Bishop George Stallings of Washington DC, to name a few.

Churches have both the resources and the spiritual component to enhance the group dynamics. Through including the Christian principle of healing and wholeness, both psychological and spiritual healing can take place. This is directly related to the ministry of Jesus and subsequently the ministry of the church as well. There is a priestly dimension of the church found in the ministry of Jesus that expounds, "The role of a priest is to provide comfort and assurance to those who are suffering or in trouble."[13] That Jesus was sent to "heal the brokenhearted" (Luke 4:18, NKJV) has special meaning to victims of sexual abuse. Thus, this form of ministry must become a priority to the black church because it was a priority to Jesus.

Stories of historical and contemporary African American heroes have a way of drawing in young black males and giving them a sense of "somebodyness" and purpose. In his book *Africentric Christianity*, author and scholar J. Deotis Roberts reminds us of the significance in historical and cultural pride, the effects it may have on black youth, and how ministry can be enhanced by the knowledge of it.[14] The concept of Afrocentrism, as mentioned earlier, can make a positive contribution to the self-esteem of young black males, thus helping to prevent risky behavior.

Exciting new possibilities are brewing within the kettles of black churches that are both willing and able to reclaim black youth. Roberts has referred to the black church as the "sleeping giant."[15] If ever there was a time when that giant should awaken, that time is now. Perhaps the pounding of a judge's gavel, the jingling of a prison guard's keys, and the slamming of jail cells that bind our youth will awaken this "giant." It has awakened in the past, and I pray it will awaken again.

The black church is particularly equipped to address this disturbing trend concerning young black males in American society. In this study we have reviewed a number of potential programs that may be implemented at a number of given churches. Community faith-based programs that involve culturally specific development can unlock the confidence of black males as belonging to a great people and at the same time teach the Christian faith message of being made in the image of God. The nature and mission of the church, rooted in the life of Jesus, dictates and demands struggling to better the quality of life for young black males—in both body and soul.

The church must be intentional about initiating key programs in their areas and working closely with schools and parents to bring about positive change. At the same time, churches must be unflaggingly committed to confronting racism and injustice as it relates to the judicial system and other social structures. We must seek not only to better conditions for black men and youth, but for the black family as well through better education, training, employment with decent wages, a safe environment, and the freedom of personal and collective expression. The black church stands at a pivotal moment in history, and the question remains, will the "sleeping giant" sleep on, or it be awakened by the cries of thousands of young black males (and females) across our nation in cribs of poverty seeking the warm milk of freedom and love? Let us pray that their cries are heard and the "sleeping giant" awakens in the form of programs and unending determination to ultimately bear witness to the gospel of Jesus and bring glory to God.

NOTES

1. Jennifer Hamer, *What It Means to be Daddy: Fatherhood for Black Men Living Away from Their Children* (New York: Columbia University Press, 2001), 22.

2. Earl O. Hutchinson, *The Assassination of the Black Male Image* (New York: Simon and Schuster, 1994), 25.

3. William Julius Wilson, *When Work Disappears* (New York: Vintage, 1997); *The Declining Significance of Race* (Chicago: University of Chicago Press, 1980).

4. John Hurst Adams, "Where Do We Go from Here?" in *Black Men in Prison*, ed. Gayraud Wilmore (Atlanta: ITC Press, 1990), 115.

5. Ibid., 154.

6. Ibid., 154.

7. Ibid., 154.

8. Andrew Billingsley, *Mighty Like a River: The Black Church and Social Reform* (New York: Oxford University Press, 1999).

9. Ibid., 107.

10. Ibid., 109.

11. Paul Hill Jr., *Coming of Age: African American Male Rites-of-Passage* (Chicago: African American Images, 1992), 90.

12. Ibid., 104.

13. J. Deotis Roberts, *Prophethood of Black Believers: An African American Political Theology for Ministry* (Louisville: Westminster John Knox Press, 1994), 2.

14. J. Deotis Roberts. *Africentric Christianity* (Valley Forge, PA: Judson, 2000).

15. In a private conversation with J. Deotis Roberts while I was a seminary student at Duke Divinity School in 2001, Roberts used the phrase "sleeping giant" to describe the church. He has alluded to this theme in several of his works, including *Africentric Christianity* and *The Prophethood of Black Believers*.

CHAPTER 6

Yield Not to Temptation: Confronting the Financial Challenges of the Black Family

MICHAEL L. COOK, MDiv

> Let no debt remain outstanding, except the
> continuing debt to love one another, for he who loves
> his fellowman has fulfilled the law (Romans 13:8, NIV).

Each of us is given a gift and a corresponding passion to pursue that gift. Most often the gift is revealed long before we recognize it as a gift or, rather, as a point of passionate interest. In my case, the interest in personal finances came when as a small child I began, innocently enough, to orient my mind and my skills around the subject. Even then it seemed that I knew the importance of creating control and placing a solid structure around one's personal financial matters. Not much has changed after all these years, which leads to the question: What can the church do to address this problem?

The financial challenges faced by black families are large and wide, and they must be dealt with now. I believe that we can make progress if we take one challenge at a time and create solutions. The black church in particular holds tremendous resources to address this problem. Unfortunately, believers are often shy and hesitate to reveal their financial woes to their church families. Both ministers and congregates have contributed to a religious culture in which people really don't want to know about another person's "money problems" because, when a problem is recognized, it means the church has to respond. Whether it is an individual, a particular ministry, or the church at large in financial trouble, it is difficult for the church to stand by and do nothing.

One of the things many churches have done and continue to do, is to hold financial planning workshops. Though seemingly a very small gesture, these events play a major role in raising consciousness about financial matters and demonstrating that there is not a contradiction between faith in Jesus Christ and successful financial management.

I grew up in a single-parent home, as many black children did at the time and continue to do today. I was raised in public housing and in a household that did not generate much income for the necessities of my mother, my brother, and me. It seemed we always had to postpone the purchase of everything, even if we needed it for survival. My mother always said, "Wait until the next payday and I will see what I can do." Unfortunately, the next payday produced the same result as the previous payday. We had plenty of love but not much money. I am sure that many of you can relate to the same scenario in your immediate family or in your extended family.

My mother worked very long and hard in a manufacturing plant for minimum wage, which, at the time, was a mere $2.15 per hour. She typically worked forty hours per week, but when the work got slow, the supervisor would inform her that her hours would be reduced. Sometimes it would reach a point where she worked only twenty hours per week, which did very little to help an already financially depressed household without any outside support.

Mother was a hardworking woman and was full of pride, always rising early for work and coming home late in the evenings, as black parents have done for generations. She would always do all that she could to make ends meet. However, over and over again the ends never met, and her cry was always the same: "I don't make enough money to take care of you and your brother." Unfortunately, many black families face the same dilemma day in and day out in this advanced society.

In looking at my mother's situation, I grew to have an appreciation for the need for control and structure around one's personal financial matters. It was hard for me to imagine that someone could work so hard and so often and have very little to show for it in terms of money. So, being an inquisitive young boy, I had a direct conversation with my mother, the kind that at some other point would have gotten my teeth knocked out. But she was a true sport in this case. One day after she had gotten in from work, we sat down at the kitchen table, and I asked her if she had a budget. She looked surprised that such a young boy would be asking such an offbeat question at that time of the day, but I really wanted to know, because I could not bear to see her continue to work and not get the full benefit of working. She paused for a moment and said, "Boy, I don't make enough money to have a budget. I make what I make, and I use it to pay for what I can, and that is that."

After a moment of contemplation, I attempted to argue that it was just not true, that anybody could have a budget no matter how much money she or he made. It was of no use. She gave me a stare that told me to shut up, and she insisted that I go and wash the dishes. I believe that this is what many black families are faced with each day of their working lives: the belief that they could not really create control and structure around their personal financial matters because of their circumstances of work and income. Oh, how history continues to repeat itself.

Though, I was not able to convince my mother to establish a system of personal financial management, I discovered that personal finances would always be an important part of life. So important, in fact, that to mismanage this area of life is in essence to mismanage one's life. Nothing that we do escapes the moving hand of personal finances. Everywhere we go and all that we do has a connection with our personal financial matters; even death is a financial matter. Therefore, financial planning is an activity we simply cannot overlook.

Much time has passed since I began this discovery from my own family, but not much has changed in black families in general. My experience has taught me that there is an ever-present weakness in the personal financial infrastructure in the black family. It is a problem that appears to be growing worse even with the rise of more "educated" blacks.

Over the past decade, I have worked in the financial services industry as a bank manager serving a primarily urban customer base that predominately consists of blacks. In this experience, I have had the opportunity to counsel countless black families and individuals on matters related to personal finances, which have not been much different from the time I attempted to talk with my mother about the matter. What has been revealed to me, over and over again, is that when it comes to personal finances, most black families are vulnerable and there are patterns of behavior that have contributed to this state of affairs.

Confronting the Barriers to Family Financial Health

I have discovered that there are a few reasons why most black family finances are out of balance. For one, we have not found consistent ways to generate sufficient income for our families. In addition, blacks generally have an enormous and insatiable appetite for spending and conspicuous consumption. Finally, there is the absence of a systematic plan of saving and planning for unexpected expenses. These factors taken into consideration offer some insight into the financial weaknesses in so many black families.

In a bank, one has the opportunity to meet virtually every type of working person, from the blue-collar factory worker to the white-collar corner office manager. Over time, you began to discover what their working lives are like outside of the bank and the income they generate from doing their jobs. In most cases, their account activity and balance generally tells a more revealing story than what they would have you believe. There are many telling signs that we are trained to evaluate to determine the health of a customer base, namely, the frequency of overdrawn accounts and the ability of the customer to apply for and receive credit.

It is generally known and accepted that Americans as a whole do not save on a regular basis, but when it comes to blacks in particular, we have a tendency to save at an even lesser rate. It is as if the concept of saving systematically is completely foreign to us. Our minds, it seems, are set on living for the moment and not preparing well for the future. The black family does not do a very good job of saving.

In many cases, the black customers I served were very weak when it came to two areas. One, their accounts were overdrawn 75 percent of the time, and even when they did bring the accounts current, it would not be long before the accounts were overdrawn again. In addition, when it came to applying for credit, black families had a difficult time acquiring standard credit for such items as homes and cars.

These customers continuously indicated that the problem they were having was the lack of income from the work they were doing. Even the customers with the "good jobs" always complained they could not make enough money to take care of their households with the jobs they had because they did not receive the promotions they deserved because of the color of their skin. I'm sure that many of you can relate to this type of situation.

In addition to these factors, we must consider the overwhelming percent of blacks who spend time on the unemployment line, continue to be relegated to jobs that are below their education and experience level, or are imprisoned only to return to society without the ability to find adequate work. In each case, it is extremely difficult to generate sufficient income to care for our black families. We must find more effective and sustainable means to generate income Lack of income is only one problem that contributes to the weakness in personal financial matters of black families. Spending and conspicuous consumption have become synonymously connected with black families as well. It is as if we have found a way to connect our value as individuals and as a group with the things that we buy, even if we do not have the income to support the purchase of the items and accessories that we gather. The black experience in slavery may have a great deal to do with this need to somehow indicate our worth by our possessions.

Others outside the black race have understood this need and arranged it as an opportunity for their gain. When you examine predominantly black neighborhoods and assess the products and services offered in these neighborhoods, more often than not, blacks are not being offered the products and services their families need.

For example, nail shops, music stores, cell phone stores, payday loan stores, banking institutions, automobile dealerships, beauty supply stores, Chinese restaurants, pawn shops, dry cleaners, and a whole host of other businesses are owned and operated by others outside the black race. They have discovered that we have a need to spend and spend, even if we as a group earn far less than other races in terms of income. Until we can find a way to get a handle on this spending behavior, the black family will continue to be challenged in regard to their personal finances.

Preparing for Retirement and Beyond

We promote a college education as a way for advancement for our children, yet we do little in terms of saving properly in advance for that education. Consequently, most black college graduates leave school with thousands upon thousands of dollars in student loan obligations. When this occurs the financial challenge for the black family begins even before sufficient income has been generated. In addition, when it comes to retirement saving, we push this obligation aside to the point that it makes us continually obligated to work even in the later years of our lives when we should be spending time supporting younger black families.

To be sure, you can go to almost any Wal-Mart on any given day and witness an elderly black person working who has retired from some organization but must continue to work to make ends meet. It is a sad case, but it is often the case. When I was in college, I had the privilege of getting to know a black security officer very well. I discovered that he was a retired executive from IBM, yet here he was working security. He made it very clear that he was working not because he wanted to but so that he could financially support his family. His situation is common. If you think about it, you know many black families in this situation. Saving systematically for retirement was something that he did not do, as is the case with so many blacks. This orientation of saving does a great deal to hurt and hinder black families in terms of personal finances.

In the case of earning sufficient income for our families, I believe that we must get back to the days when we were entrepreneurs and innovators. In other words, we need to start controlling the flow of our incomes by creating businesses that address the needs of not only blacks but other races as well. We need to take the skills that we use every day to create income for our employers and transform those skills into our own income-generating sources. For as long as our income is based on a job and someone else is controlling all the factors of that employment, we will always be short on cash. We all know people who have worked for years from sunup to sundown and have had very little success in making ends meet for their families with enough money left over to save for the future.

Taming the Desire to Spend

We need to find more productive ways of addressing our spending behavior. In my opinion, spending is a psychological problem that can be addressed as any other psychological problem. In general, it is a stigma in the black community to receive counseling for mental behavior, but it is certainly necessary if we are to get a handle on this spending challenge.

In these medical sessions, we can began to undercover the motivation behind our spending craze and develop alternative solutions that can provide the same relief that spending does without having to constantly purchase. To believe that spending is anything other than psychological would be to deceive oneself.

Much of the problem of systematically saving for the future can all but be addressed if we began to possess our own businesses and address our spending behavior. Consider this. If a black family is generating sufficient income and controlling that income, then is it not reasonable to believe that the family could establish a plan that would prepare them for a more financially secure future. We will also need to continue to gain knowledge and understanding of personal financial matters through books, seminars, and personal experience.

If we don't, the future will find black families broke and frustrated. I conclude with a few suggestions for churches and groups to consider in their ministry to the financial needs to families.

Strategies for Churches

1. Develop an economic development ministry that helps to promote homeownership, savings, investments, and entrepreneurships.
2. Form partnerships with existing organizations like HUD Homes, Habitat for Humanity, and FHA to encourage homeownership. Homeownership is one of the most successful paths toward building a family's economic security. ·
3. Establish a credit union at your church to provide low-interest

or no-interest loans to start small businesses, short-term investments, invest in real estate, etc.

Strategies for Families

1. Be honest about your financial situation. Organize a budget that reflects the family's long-range and short-range goals. It may be challenging at first, but stick to it!

2. Attend local homeownership and real estate investment seminars. In most communities, city municipal offices will often sponsor economic development workshops. These are excellent opportunities to do your homework about the most viable financial opportunities that may be available in your community.

3. Start a small business. Too often black families have neglected this lost art. There are any number of small businesses that require very little start-up capital yet can reap huge rewards if pursued. Establishing a business is an excellent way to build a family legacy that can continue to provide economic support to families for generations to come. The local library has countless numbers of books and resources that can help you get started.

CHAPTER 7

Models for Ministry to Black Families

JOHNNY B. HILL, PhD

Therefore, since we are surrounded by so great a cloud
of witnesses, let us also lay aside every weight and the
sin that clings so closely, and let us run with perseverance
the race that is set before us, looking to Jesus the pioneer
and perfecter of our faith, who for the sake of the joy
that was set before him endured the cross, disregarding
its shame, and has taken his seat at the right hand
of the throne of God. (Hebrews 12:1-2, NRSV)

Although the challenges confronting African American family life seem daunting, there is much cause to celebrate. Countless churches, individuals, groups, nonprofits, and social service agencies are doing amazing work with families. Often this work goes unacknowledged in the mainstream media. But none of us can escape the continuous onslaught of negative statistics and reports concerning African American families. If one simply accepted these reports, it could easily lead to a scourge of hopelessness and despair. However, because of the faithful and courageous witness of persons in communities everywhere, African American families continue to press on in a spirit of resiliency and possibility.

The purpose of this chapter is simply to share some models or examples of ministries to African American families. Not all African American families are the same. Therefore, no one model will work for all congregations, individuals, or groups. Selecting the right strategy for a particular person or group will depend in large measure on goals, objectives, resources, and other particularities. We can, however, glean some insights from ministries that have enjoyed a measure of faithfulness in their efforts. After surveying a number of ministries across the nation, I have identified a few that differ in their approach, demographics, and overall scope.

The following models are only snapshots of the multitude of the possibilities available for ministry to families. One needs only to go online or contact a local family resource center for potential strategies. The first step in the process is taking a serious, introspective appraisal of what is already happening in the church or community. Are there any opportunities for partnerships? How can your ministry to families complement existing efforts? An example would be if there are churches in your community already offering a child development program. Is there still a need, or should you pursue other areas of need?

The effectiveness of a particular ministry will depend largely on the question of whether the ministry is meeting an expressed need in the community. While there are a number of strategies and approaches to consider, some insight may be gathered from the brief survey of models that follow.

Afrocentric Approach
Trinity United Church of Christ, Chicago
Since the late sixties and early seventies, a number of churches have tried to integrate an Afrocentric approach to the way they do ministry. Trinity United Church of Christ has made such an attempt and thrived in doing so for more than thirty years.

Located in the heart of Chicago's Southside, Dr. Jeremiah Wright has injected a thematic focus of being "unashamedly black and unapologetically Christian" to involve all ministries of the church, including families. The church has a large urban congregation that has developed a very well-known married couples ministry. Its mission statement indicates it is "a fellowship of couples aiming to strengthen our marriages, while providing and receiving support from other couples."[1] Among some of its many programs are the married couples' conference, marriage retreat, date night, and the marriage ministry picnic. By specifically dealing with the issue of marriage, Trinity's ministry has created the space for couples to share experiences, resources, insights, and stories. In many cases, a wealth of expertise can be shared when couples find the room to share their joys, triumphs, struggles, and achievements as a couple in a loving, supporting, and spiritually affirming atmosphere. Trinity has also demonstrated a commitment to outreach efforts. This is a very important component to any church ministry to families. The church must seek to minister outwardly as it continues to equip inwardly.

In many churches, the idea of organizing their programs in such a way as to invite and attract individuals who are not members has been a difficult undertaking. Typically, a culture develops within a particular ministry where the individuals and couples begin to build trust, mutual respect, and meaningful dialogue. The temptation is to keep a "good thing" within the confines of the group. Although it is important to encourage and nurture that sense of group cohesion, it is also critical that the ministry remains mission and purpose driven. It must seek to live out a covenantal relationship rooted in God yet shared and modeled for others. Trinity, through its conferences, retreats, date nights, and other activities, has opened the door for couples to share in this meaningful interaction while they may be at different stages in their marriage or Christian faith journey.

Models for Ministry to Black Families

The Partnership Approach
Second Baptist Church, Evanston, Illinois

As a rural congregation on the outskirts of Chicago's North Shore, Second Baptist Church has developed a family ministry program that is multiracial and intergenerational. Rev. Mark A. Dennis Jr., former president of the nonprofit consulting firm the Alford Group has become a passionate advocate of the "partnership" approach. Rather than starting programs from the ground up, Rev. Dennis has encouraged his members to seek out partnerships with existing organizations, such as Metropolitan Family Services, the American Cancer Society, and Lawrence Hall Youth Services, as pathways to effective ministry for families and individuals. I find this approach especially compelling considering the fact that there are a number of existing organizations with specific areas of expertise that are doing exceptional work across the country.

Adopting a partnership approach not only saves the church resources, it also maximizes ministry efforts and contributes to a sustained ministry over the long haul. Of course the concern that many have with this approach is that partnering with organizations may not guarantee that another organization shares the vision and ethos of the church, group, or individuals involved. This is a very critical factor to consider. After all, many pastors, lay leaders, and individuals want to ensure that whatever is done is advancing the mission and vision that God has given. At the same time, through careful research and effective relationship building, there is often a middle ground that can be established if parties involved concentrate on strengthening the family.

Some of the programs and initiatives Rev. Dennis's family ministry has engaged in are conferences, retreats, special dinners, anniversary celebrations, and family fun nights. Many of their programs are geared toward involving the larger family unit, not just parents or children, but grandparents, aunts, uncles, cousins, and friends. It is important to remember that nearly 70 percent of African American households are headed by a single parent, which means that the extended family is critical to the success and viability of family life. The obvious strength of Second Baptist Church's programs is in their focus on reaching out to the extended family and forming meaningful partnerships with existing organizations.

Educational Approach
White Rock Baptist Church, Durham, North Carolina
A number of churches have decided that one of the best ways to reach out to families is through Christian education. After all, education has been a staple in the African American community and continues to be an important strategy. White Rock Baptist Church, considered an urban southern congregation, is located about three miles south of North Carolina Central University in Durham, North Carolina. Many of the founders of White Rock Baptist Church established a number of major businesses, including North Carolina Mutual Insurance, Inc. An affluent congregation with a mixed membership, ministry to families often involves a series of education-related programs, including workshops, seminars, spiritual retreats, and small group ministries. Its focus is on "family relationships" and "growth." They wisely focus on relationships that allow them to interpret family in a number of ways. They seek therapeutic and preventive approaches by working collaboratively with married, divorced, single, engaged, widowed, elderly, and young members of the church and community.

Too often churches readily embrace ministry to youth but are quite hesitate about ministry to others who either don't fit the ideal family model or who fall out of the purview of a two-parent family household. Why this approach is so important is that most youth are living in single-parent households, which are often led by a single sibling, aunt, grandmother, or other extended family member. Simply focusing on one population within a family structure (youth, mothers, fathers, etc.) is significant, but ministry needs to seek a more holistic approach through conversation, interaction, and relationship building.

The strengths of the White Rock Baptist Church program can be found in its ability to promote loving, nurturing, and authentic interactions between family members. Its attention to education is extremely important as well, because it seeks to provide training, education, and ongoing spiritual formation opportunities; subsequently, it is able to make a significant difference within the congregation and wider community. Looking more outwardly and considering mentoring opportunities for families who would value the same types of educational exposure could strengthen this program.

Creative Approaches to Marriage Counseling
Personal Transformations, Royal Oak, Michigan

Founded by Melva Thomas and Jesse Johnson, Personal Transformations is a program that uses creative approaches to help married couples and families. The uniqueness of Personal Transformations is that Thomas and Johnson, as therapists, are intentional about helping couples struggle with inner attitudes, thoughts, perceptions, feelings, and behaviors as a pathway to a strong and healthy relationship. Using their own marriage of more than 28 years as a case study, Thomas and Johnson have worked with churches, faith-based programs, couples, families, and individuals.

Personal Transformations emphasizes the importance for couples to confront their underlying psychological and personal historical issues in order to move toward healthy relationships. Considering the deep sense of superficiality that is a reality in many of our churches, the Johnsons' program is challenging yet undeniably essential. Most couples find it difficult to be honest about the nature of their relationship in the church community. Afraid of being exposed, many go on in quiet agony, concealing the problems of their marriage and family life. What the Johnsons have attempted to do with Personal Transformations, and their accompanying organization, the Johnson Relationship Institute, is to show that understanding oneself is as important to a healthy relationship as understanding one's spouse and other family members.

Social Action Approach
Allen Temple Church, Los Angeles

Some congregations have sought to deal with the challenges and struggles of African American family life through social action and political advocacy. J. Alfred Smith Sr., pastor of Allen Temple Church, has done just that. Two nonprofit organizations, the Family Life Center and the Allen Temple Economic Develop-ment and Housing Corporation, have sought to treat both the spiritual and material realities of African American family life. In addition to its Couples Enrichment Ministry, which offers premarital courses and biblical and spiritual education about marriage, the church also offers housing for seniors and families affected by HIV/AIDS. An often-neglected area of family ministry is the more difficult task of broaching the social, economic, and political realities of poverty, incarceration, health care, housing, and public education. Historically, the black church has understood that the realities of racial and economic exploitation have deeply impacted family relationships. To overlook this important fact would be to bypass the complexity of ministry to families. Ministry to African American families is a war that must be waged on many fronts. Indeed, one of those is dealing with the social issues at work in African American family life. Smith's church has done an exceptional job of ministering to the spirit and the body of families in its congregation.

Models for Ministry to Black Families

Programmatic Approach
The Family Reunion Institute
Temple University, Philadelphia

For more than seventeen years, the Family Reunion Institute of Temple University has been promoting and encouraging families, churches, civic organizations, and others to recover the vibrancy of family reunions. The institute was established in 1990 by Dr. Ione D. Vargus with the purpose of strengthening the extended family. Dr. Vargus recognized, as did many other researchers, that the extended family has provided enormous resources for the resilience of African American families. Informal adoptions, shared resources, childcare, discipline, and shared parenting are all part of the realities of the extended family. The tradition of family reunions has been a hallmark in African American family life. Through family reunions, family bonds are renewed, new relationships are established, and family history is shared and celebrated. Black churches have a particularly unique role to play because of the prominence they hold in family life. The church can be a powerful conduit to promoting and helping families organize a family reunion of their own. Although most family reunions do require some funding, churches can help families find creative ways of paying for their reunions through fund-raising, potlucks, and so on.

Black Marriage Day
Wedded Bliss Foundation, Washington, DC

One of the many movements attracting a great deal of attention nationally is the Black Marriage Day. Nisa Islam Muhammad and Jennifer Muhammad organized the Wedded Bliss Foundation, based in Washington, DC, to begin to raise consciousness about the joys and blessings of married life. Growing out of the premise that married people live longer, fare better financially, and contribute to stronger communities and youth achievement, they began promoting the fourth Sunday in March as Black Marriage Day. It is considered an annual day of celebrating marriage and married people. This is an excellent program that can be easily appropriated by churches with little or no financial commitment but that affirms and validates marital relationships in the church and community.

One of the significant aspects of the Black Marriage Day program is that anyone—a family, individual, couple, church, school, or business—can participate in this worthwhile campaign. An inevitable drawback to this type of program is that persons who are single, divorced, or widowed may harbor bitter feelings about marriage itself and find this program offensive or annoying. Here is where it is important to recognize and celebrate *difference*. Pastors, lay leaders, and individuals engaged in family ministry must be able to celebrate the particularities of all individuals or groups. Celebrating one (e.g., married couples) does not in any way demean or negate the experiences of others. As persons made in the image of God, the church can celebrate wherever a person may be in his or her Christian journey.

Conclusion

The examples mentioned here are merely snapshots of the many possibilities for ministry in a particular local congregation or group. There is no one-size-fits-all approach to developing a dynamic family ministry. What is perhaps most important is the commitment, faith, and passion of individuals willing to pursue the difficult task of leadership. New models are being developed daily as churches and faithful individuals continue to seek creative ways to promote healthy families in their congregations. With each model, however, there are shared constants: (1) a desire to strengthen African American family life, (2) the courage to be creative, and (3) the commitment to sustain their efforts over time. Without question, developing a viable family ministry in the church is not at all easy. Chances are it will require significant funds, countless hours, and painstaking planning and organizing. In the final analysis, however, there is reassurance in knowing that lives will be changed, communities transformed, and spirits renewed. Know that the Spirit of Jesus Christ is at work in the ministries and models we seek to explore. As Fred Lofton, former president of the Progressive National Baptist Convention, observed years ago, "The family becomes the agent for teaching its members [Christian community] to exhibit faith, hope, love, self-confidence, self-respect, self-esteem, self-pride, honesty, trust, and a fear of God."[2] Without question, it is within the context of the family that the grace and love of God are lived out and made visible every day. By strengthening the family through planning and developing sound models, we enrich the faith and spiritual journey of believers. Finally, we also bear witness to God's goodness in the world in which we are called to live out our faith.

NOTES

1. http://www.tucc.org/married_couples.htm.

2. Fred Lofton, "Teaching Christian Values," in *The Black Family: Past, Present, and Future,* ed. Lee N. June and Matthew Parker (Grand Rapids: Zondervan, 1991), 127.

CHAPTER 8

Practical Steps for Ministry to Black Families in Today's World

ELIZABETH JOHNSON WALKER, PhD

From time to time God comes along and invites us to experience a new diet. For the Hebrew children God did that in the wilderness when he fed human beings food from heaven and slaked their thirst with water gushing from a rock in the desert. The African American/Black family at various times in the journey have come across new experiences and seen and heard things never seen or heard before, new things captured the imaginations and served to move toward ever-increasing imagination and creativity.

For Easter people the death and resurrection of Jesus the Christ points toward new beginnings in relationships made possible by Grace. We discern spiritual resources that will carry us through and change our diet. We remember that God has forgotten our disgrace, and Grace reminds of that we are a people with a future.

(Sermon excerpt, Joshua 5, March 2004,
Elizabeth J. Walker)

The reality of African American families in today's world has been shaped by historical and sociocultural experiences and events of African Americans under the impact of patriarchy in American culture, from slavery to the present. The emphasis on race discrimination is an important factor to consider when identifying and responding to the spiritual needs of this population. The instance and depth of suffering are often inextricable consequences of cultural and social location and race discrimination.

A challenge of the church community is to develop ministry that is adequate to respond to the spiritual condition of African American families. These sources must assist in the discernment process and in coming to terms with what it means to share a particular history.

In my analysis of the African American family, several shared themes emerge:

1. The historical Ancient African heritage where the oldest human skeletal remains were excavated
2. Ancient Egyptian black legacy of family and the value of each member of the family
3. Acculturation and the legacy of estranged relationships as consequence of patriarchal institutes of race discrimination in America
4. The sustaining character of spirituality from ancient black African legacy to the present
5. The relational nature of personality development and its embeddedness in social relations

These points indicate that African Americans share genetic history with other human beings, have integrity and value, suffer conditions of discrimination and estrangement, share the legacy of spirituality as a salient value and strength, and have potential to thrive in relationships of integrity with others.

Spirituality has served as a strategy that has supported the African American family's need to have integrity in relationships and to promote personal growth across time and across generations. Estrangement in relationships serves to interrupt spirituality. While the pervasive patterns of race discrimination have been brought to bear on the African American family in today's world, spirituality continues to be a locus and resource for meaning and value in relations. The black church and oral tradition have functioned to support and perpetuate the heritage and legacy of spirituality in African American families. It is essential that this very important resource and strength be conceptualized and nurtured in the family. Further, it is also essential to acknowledge that the configuration and stressors of today's black family have changed. The challenges that face the church are enhanced by the changing configuration.

The configuration of the black family has changed tremendously since the middle of the twentieth century. There has been a decline in marriage but not a decline in long-term romantic relationships among African Americans adults. Life expectancy has increased. African American women participate as a majority in the community of faith. African American women living with HIV/AIDS is on the rise, aggravated by the inaccessibility of medical care and social services. The community of faith is struggling with the question of sexual preference and its implications for ministry. Violence and abuse in families is increasingly a concern. The instance of our children in single-parent households, with grandparents, in foster care and in other institutional settings is on the rise. Increased poverty and homelessness have placed many of our children at risk for chronic poverty and out-of-home placement. There are unique challenges for our families across the life cycle. Any attempt to support families must consider the multigenerational concerns as well as spiritual.

Black family resiliency in the face of such challenges has always been supported in some ways by social and church programs. The black church has functioned as a place of spiritual identity and formation with programs to support their populations and as a place for networking with social services. Historically ministers in the black church served, among other things, as resources for counseling and information that connected the community to services. Education was, and is, a strong value that reinforced spiritual formation. Education served the need to make visible resources in the community that supported the family.

Today's African American family must continue to be resilient. There is a real need for education to (1) assist in self-definition, spirituality, vision, and purpose; and (2) make visible resources in the church and the community that may assist the black family in attaining its goals.

Practical Steps for Developing Ministry Strategies

The focus of this chapter is to offer practical steps for ministry with African American/black families. The first step is to reclaim the heritage and legacy of spirituality that places value on each individual and on the family as blessed by God and therefore a recipient of grace. Many organizations have developed programs for the family. The unique resource of the church with an explicit vision of caring for the soul and attending to the integrity of the human creation is found in the mission of the *beloved* community. The first step involves two things, (1) identify the ministry leadership and (2) provide education. The second step involves five things (1) gather the community to evoke the power of God to discern the nature of the program(s); (2) develop, resource, and implement program(s) that arise during the discerning process; (3) network with other church and community programs; (4) access programs; and (5) explore funding options if necessary. I will limit the focus of this chapter to explore steps in developing and supporting a spirituality that turns toward faith and its resources.

The Ministry Leadership

The social and political focus of the church is not necessarily linked to the ministry needs of the African American families in their communities. In my experience as pastor, professor, and clinician working with African American ministers and families, I find that there is often a poverty of experience in regard to a person's ability to make a clear connection between personal, social, cultural, and spiritual meaning. In other words, what does my faith have to do with my life? This is a question that is grappled with by leadership and laypeople, and it is a fundamental question. The church as organizational system and the African American families whom they serve have similar experiences of a loss for words in matters of spirituality. This is a spiritual formation concern.

One spiritual focus of the church is to address this ambiguity with the concept of the beloved community with leaders of faith. The beloved community, and the concept of faith leaders, suggests the tradition of spirituality in which every person has value and a role. This brings to mind principles of the New Testament church where the leaders were very intentional about the common and spiritual welfare of families and individuals in the families.

Important to note is that those leaders of the church had been given sufficient preparation for leadership in their various roles. Historically, persons in ministry leadership were

- grounded in a tradition with theological and ethical framework
- able to conceptualize and grasp a spiritual experience
- possessed of maturity and integrity
- clear about their defined roles and limits
- accountable for their actions

The vision and focus of ministry was to create and care for the beloved community. Beloved community faith activity evoked the revelation of God and reason.

Ministry leadership assumes adequate preparation for the ministry task and a plan of self-care. Ministry leadership models spirituality and self-care to families and individuals. This process also provides a source that assists in the ongoing integration of faith with experience.

Questions for the Ministry Leadership

1. Why is it important to integrate one's faith commitments with one's leadership style? How do you attempt to do so?

2. Do the leaders of your community balance community care with self-care? If yes, how? If no, why not? How may you model self-care for your families?

3. What opportunities are there for families to support one another? What focused support groups exist beyond Sunday school and Bible study opportunities? Who attends to networking, and how is that done?

4. What is the configuration of families in your community? What are the critical concerns of your families with children? Aging families? Blended families? Families with chronic illness? Families living with disabilities, poverty, homelessness, or legal problems? What about at-risk populations?

5. What are you doing about advocacy?

6. How much quality time do you spend with your families? How much time do your families spend with one another? What tools are used to gather ongoing feedback from the community in regard to the appropriateness of existing and planned programs? What studies assist you to respond to the social needs of your community?

Educate Our African American Children and Youth

"Train children in the right way, and when old, they will not stray" (Proverbs 22:6, NRSV).

The African American church has historically been a place of education. Sunday school and Bible study are the context in which our children and youth come to know their spiritual heritage as a faith journey. Reflections on experiences of faith—in Bible stories, in the lives of others, and in their own contexts—are ways in which children and youth come to know their spiritual heritage and legacy. A consistent diet of spiritual formation in the church and in the community has the potential to influence value systems and choices. It also serves to connect the children and youth to their roles in community and to contribute toward the development of character and self-esteem.

An important variable in the development of self-esteem is to have a clearly defined understanding of oneself and one's value in the family and in the community of faith. Children and youth must be encouraged to (1) voice their experiences, (2) participate in youth-led explorations of meaning and celebration, and (3) participate in community, outreach, and youth group projects of advocacy as expressions of their shared legacy.

Questions for Our Children and Youth Ministry
1. How does your community affirm the gifts of your children and youth?
2. Who evokes the voice of your children and youth in program development?
3. How are children and youth socialized for leadership? Who does this?
4. Do you teach children and youth spiritual disciplines? Why or why not?
5. How is the wisdom of children held in the community?
6. What issues and challenges are important to your children and youth? What is different and what is similar about working with children and youth versus with adults?

These questions are suggestions for initiating a dialogue within the community that acknowledges and includes the voice of children and youth's self-experience in the conceptualization and development of programs.

Caring for the African American Family

In this section I will respond specifically to the pastoral care needs of families who approach ministry leaders for intervention for a variety of reasons. Pastoral care involves attending to any counseling needs that may arise. Pastoral counseling is a professional activity that is the function of a professional, licensed, behavior-care provider and is different from the pastoral care provided by the ministry leadership. Pastoral counseling is sometimes indicated, and for those occasions the ministry leadership should identify a professional pastoral counselor within the community and be familiar with referral sources to include sliding scale fees, any available free services, and social service programs.

It is important for ministry leaders to acknowledge their own limitations in regard to time commitments, orientation, and training and to develop an ongoing network of referral sources to ensure that the emotional and psychological needs are attended to, should those needs occur. In the interest of self-care for the community as a whole, practical consideration should be given to the process by which pastoral care and pastoral counseling referrals are attended to.

In my experience families often seek the ministry leadership for counseling assistance with couple and family concerns. Discover what counseling, workshop, training opportunities, and services are available in your community. Visit the workshop leaders and service providers to understand their philosophy and the appropriateness of existing opportunities and services for your own community referral bank. See what others have done and what is available in your area.

An important resource for the ministry leadership team that will assist in the process of developing appropriate counseling tools to be used for couples and families is the PREPARE/ ENRICH Training Seminar. This training is available to ministry leaders and provides premarital and marital inventories to guide couples toward their goals of communication, setting realistic goals, conflict resolution, budgeting, and many other important concerns that couples bring to the counseling setting. The inventory also includes a way to look at spirituality. This training and inventory is an invaluable way for ministry leadership teams who may not have the time to sit in a formal counseling program but who desire some expertise to support the counseling needs of families in a time-limited manner.

In program development with African American families, it is important to develop some assessment tools to discern what the community needs are. There are Internet sources that have posted their strategies for building and enhancing family ministries, such as those available from the African American Healthy Family Initiative (www.acf.hhs.gov), African American Family Life Education (www.aafle.org), and the Anne E. Casey Foundation (www.aecf.org). Professional consultants are available to assist in program building efforts. During the discerning process the ministry leadership might consider creating a family needs survey to identify the following:

■ configuration of families in the community
■ marital stressors
■ family stressors
■ parenting challenges
■ spiritual nurturing needs
■ premarital counseling needs
■ leadership
■ ability to host and lead community-related interest
■ ability to partner with existing programs, churches, and services

It is also important to explore intentionally those concerns and stressors affecting at-risk populations. Those populations include youth, the elderly, substance abusers, and individuals or families experiencing phase-of-life transitions, financial hardships, or chronic illness. Other at-risk groups include victims of violence, the mentally ill, refugees (whether legal or not), the homeless, the incarcerated and their families, and the LGBT (lesbian, gay, bisexual, transsexual) community. A family needs survey will assist the ministry team as it begins to prioritize program planning, mobilize resources, and develop leadership for programs.

Networking

Develop a network bank. Networking is an important function of the ministry leadership in the church community. The ministry leadership must be intentional in its efforts to develop and nurture relationships within the community. The following represent some suggestions for negotiating network contacts with the local community for the purpose of programming:

- advocacy groups and programs
- community health center
- families in your extended community of faith
- ecumenical opportunities and programs
- county mental health facilities and programs
- ministerial alliances
- mayor's breakfast

In addition to establishing networking opportunities, congregations can pursue a number of specific programs and activities. Churches can encourage family units and family leadership units to host community-related interests; to facilitate family visitation that includes extracurricular events with children and youth; and to support families in developing a community project as a group. Community service projects, such as volunteering at soup kitchens, HIV/AIDs awareness events, homeless shelters, Habitat for Humanity builds, and the like can have a tremendous impact on communities in addition to building family relationships. Developing family-oriented events that include the larger community (e.g., seminars, training events, thematic workshops) are also wonderful ways to promote family interaction and community service all at once. Congregations might also explore ways of creating mission opportunities for multiple-family participation. Other church-sponsored family activities may involve reading clubs, training events, and workshops devoted to education and strategies focused on building leaders within families and groups as well.

Some Resources to Get Started

The following resources represent thoughtful research and reflection on the plight of today's black family. Some of these resources have developed well-defined and tested strategies for responding to the churches' tasks to minister to the spiritual and social needs of families. These resources serve as an introduction to the many voices that have contributed to the definition of the problem of developing strong ministries for our African American families today.

Anderson, Herbert, and Freda A. Gardner, *Living Alone.* Louisville: Westminster John Knox, 1997.

Billingsley, Andrew. *Climbing Jacob's Ladder.* New York: Simon and Schuster, 2004.

Carter, Les, and Frank Minirth. *The Anger Workbook for Christian Parents.* San Francisco: Jossey-Bass, 2004.

Hewlett, Sylvia Ann, and Cornell West. *The War against Parents.* New York: Mariner, 1998.

June, Lee N., and Matthew Parker, eds. *The Black Family: Past, Present, and Future.* Grand Rapids: Zondervan, 1991.

Patterson, Sheron C. *Put On Your Crown: A Back Woman's Guide to Living Single.* Cleveland, OH: Pilgrim, 2006.

Richardson, Ronald W. *Creating a Healthier Church: Family Systems Theory, Leadership, and Congregational Life.* Minneapolis: Fortress Press, 1996.

Smith, Wallace Charles. *The Church in the Life of the Black Family.* Valley Forge, PA: Judson, 1985.

Walker, Elizabeth J. "Pastoral Counseling with Some African American Women." Unpublished dissertation. Atlanta: Interdenominational Theological Center, 2000.

Wigger, J. Bradley. *Together We Pray: A Prayer Book for Families.* St. Louis, MO: Chalice, 2005.

Wimberly, Anne Streaty, ed. *Keeping It Real: Working with Today's Black Youth.* Nashville: Abingdon, 2005.

Wimberly, Edward P. *Pastoral Counseling and Spiritual Values: A Black Point of View.* Nashville: Abingdon, 1982.

CHAPTER 9

Revisiting the Church in the Life of the Black Family: Then and Now

WALLACE CHARLES SMITH, DMin

In 1985 I wrote a book entitled *The Church in the Life of the Black Family*. Now, more than twenty years after its debut, many of the same problems facing families still exist—and indeed, in most instances, they have become worse.

Over the past two decades we have seen the devastating effects on families of Reagonomics and the explosion of a hip-hop sexuality that routinely defamed and denigrated women as little more than sex toys. Unwed pregnancies are epidemic, in spite of the growing fortunes of middle-class blacks, while poverty, crime, violence, drug abuse, and recreational sex are at all-time highs. Subtle language changes signal major philosophical shifts. In the 1940s and 50s, guys were "cats," sometimes even "cool cats." Today young men routinely greet each other with "What up, dawg!" We have gone from being cats to dogs, and although many of us never considered the implications, the change signaled a shift that men were now celebrating an identity as unapologetic sexual predators.

When the book was published, I argued that the secret of emotional health for black families was economic parity. That conviction remains firm, because when economic factors are on par, black families display the same percentages of functionality as whites, Asians, or Hispanics. However, the unique circumstances facing black America then and now require a broader, more expansive solution. For black families to be whole, several factors must be considered. Economics is one of those factors, but there are historic realities to understand, as well as social-psychological, physical-medical, and spiritual dimensions to be promoted and shared. And it is still my belief that the church is the vehicle where these dimensions can be best addressed.

Historical–Cultural

The black family sits in the historical and cultural realities of slavery, reconstruction, and Jim Crow segregation. We emerged in a world where blacks had few if any rights that whites were bound to respect. At the harbor in Annapolis, Maryland, there is a statue of Kunta Kinte, an ancestor of Alex Haley and the legendary African who was caught, captured, and brought to the New World. Once in the New World, he was forced to change his name and was physically mutilated when he persisted in trying to escape.

Numerous such pilgrimages from life as free black Africans to a world of brutality and incarceration comprise the reality out of which African American families evolved. When it comes to wholeness and health, the African American family system must come to grips with a history that routinely decreed a whole people to be without dignity and self-determination. Most of us over the age of forty went through school without so much as a whisper about the background or cultures of the African continent. We spent months covering Greece and Rome, entire spring semesters focused on Europe, and the last week or so centered on China and Latin America. Little, if anything, was shared about the richness of the history, customs, and culture of Africa. What we learned of the great continent came from *Tarzan* movies, where we observed one white man organizing the land's animals to destroy and defeat tribes of evil blacks, of which a few noble and loyal native bearers were notable exceptions to the majority who were portrayed as vicious cannibals.

For centuries African American families grew up believing they were inferior because of skin color, hair texture, and facial features. Cornell West, in his book *Prophesy Deliverance! An Afro-American Revolutionary Christianity*, pointed out that the history of colonialism rested on pseudoscience, which theorized that by assessing skull angles, cranium size, and slopes of foreheads, one could prove physiologically that African peoples were inferior and therefore needed to be subdued and colonized for their own good.

False, inadequate, and insufficient history is largely why in 1933 Carter G. Woodson spoke of the "miseducation of the Negro" as one of the most formidable hurdles facing black America. In spite of advances in scholarship and African American history curricula, miseducation persists. What was true in 1933 and 1985 is still regrettably true now.

Churches must organize aggressively and intentionally to set the record straight. Educational opportunities abound in church school and Bible studies. At the Shiloh Baptist Church of Washington DC, every fifth Sunday we partner with the Association for the Study of African American Life and History (ASALH) to offer a black history lesson in the Sunday school. We must help our children and youth as well as our adults to understand that we as a people came from rich and varied backgrounds. Trading centers such as Timbuktu in Mali were renowned throughout the world. Egypt was a great society when the Greeks were still wearing face paint and worshipping animals.

As a part of my fifteenth pastoral anniversary at Shiloh, we observed what we called an elder's gala. We honored 116 people who were eighty years old and older. We placed their biographies in the church newsletter. We crowned the oldest man and woman as Elders King and Queen. And all of this was an attempt to show our congregation how much we value and reverence our history.

We can also learn much from the traditions and history of Israel. God gave the Ten Commandments as the guiding principles to help Israel manage their freedom once released from Egyptian bondage. Throughout Israel's periods of independence and defeat, it is notable that the people always performed well, fought admirably, and triumphed mightily *when they recalled their venerated history*. Yet while attempting to refurbish the temple, King Josiah discovered the Book of the Law, which had been lost so long that the ancient festivals and feasts were no longer practiced. When we are cut off from our history, we lose our sense of future.

When Israel was in bondage in Babylon, prophets such as Isaiah reminded the people that there was a world beyond Babylon—because God was a God of history. The same God who could dry up the sea could and would provide the needed abilities to overcome the problems of the present.

Cornell West, in his book *Race Matters*, points out that much of the nihilism of the present, which is so pervasive among the young, is the result of the belief that life is not going anywhere. To offset this destructive belief, we must recapture our history and teach it as an example of what God has already done and what God continues to do.

I mentioned our elder's gala, which we held in our family life center. In that center we have a banquet hall known as Heritage Hall. One whole wall is covered with the pictures of those who have been honored. Our expectation is that adults will tell children the stories of their parents, how they sacrificially worked several jobs, suffered indignities and insults, but still ensured that their children inherited a better way of life.

My grandmother was a diminutive woman, not quite five feet tall. She lived to be nearly 100 years old. My earliest recollections are of her strength and courage. We lived near a railroad track, and once a huge snake came down off the tracks and slid in front of us. Without blinking an eye, my grandmother took her heel and crushed its head. She was a tough lady. She had hands like sandpaper from the years she had chopped wood on the railroad. She worked as a maid in her later years. When she went to her job cleaning rich folks' houses, she wore a black uniform with a white hat and apron. I only saw one picture of her in that uniform. On Sunday, however, she had another uniform. She was chair of the mothers' board at our home church. We have tons of pictures of her in that uniform. When she went to church, my grandmother was free. She could shout and praise the Lord because, regardless of the forces that oppressed, she served a God who was a liberator. This God was not outside the furnace putting people in, but inside the furnace getting people out. Knowledge of history is a ticket to family liberation.

Social-Psychological

Second, there is the social–psychological dimension. I use this phrase to describe all the emotional baggage that we drag around with us. Toni Morrison, in her book *The Bluest Eye*, describes little Pecola Breedlove, a black little girl who fantasizes about being white. Her fantasies eventually destroy her.

Self-hatred undercuts the lives of black families. Alcohol, drug abuse, and sexual promiscuity all come out of the roots of self-hatred. Violence results from hating the images we have of ourselves. Neighborhoods that are dilapidated are breeding grounds for the deep psychological sicknesses that make us lash out at each other. In Washington DC, children routinely write essays about preparing their funeral programs because they believe they will not live to see adulthood. West says in *Race Matters* that without a sense of life getting better, we become uncaring. We believe we have no future—that life is not going anywhere. Without direction or hope, we wind up living for the moment. Bling-bling, designer jackets and sneakers, and big SUVs are all life is. I will never get these things from flipping burgers at Wendy's, so I will get a pistol and take what I want, because *now* is the only time I can count on.

Unfortunately, some of our pietistic "by-and-by, pie-in-the-sky" theology doesn't help the situation. Indeed, we make it worse. As Jesse Jackson once said, "I don't want pie in the sky by-and-by. I want some ham where I am."

Marian Wright Edelman has said, "Hope is the best contraceptive." The greatest cure for nihilism and self-hatred is a restored future. Too many children start down the pathway of self-hatred because (1) they live in squalid, ugly surroundings; (2) they have been tracked from an early age as marginally educable; and (3) they have been traumatized by the violence and hatred they have seen all too often. Violence is a two-edged sword. Witnessing it stirs us up and thrills us. But the more we see it, the more it deadens our sense of horror.

In the fourth century, St. Augustine wrote about a Christian convert who, after his conversion, opposed the violence of the Roman gladiatorial arena. To be social, perhaps yielding to peer pressure, he attended a game with some friends. He kept his eyes closed, determined not to watch, until a particularly loud cheer caused him to open his eyes to see what the commotion was about. He saw all the blood and could not take his eyes off the carnage. He was hooked.

Witnessing violence makes those who watch it more, not less, violent. We live in a *Rambo, Terminator, Blade Runner* world, where extreme fighting has replaced the World Wrestling Federation as the gladiatorial combat of choice. The average American witnesses countless acts of violence on television daily. Studies point out that witnessing fantasy violence increases the proclivity of people to performance violent acts themselves.

That being the case, imagine the effect of witnessing real violence. It is unimaginable to consider what children experience when they see real brains blown all over the street, real corpses with unrecognizable faces because those faces have been shot off in acts of revenge. A study done at the University of Alabama pointed to the fact that low-income African American males between ages 7 and 18 are more likely to be victims of and witnesses to violence. Although women were not victimized as often and witnessed violence less frequently, the symptoms of post traumatic stress disorder (PTSD) were more extreme among them. Regression analysis revealed that being victimized and witnessing violence were also significant factors in the *reporting* of PTSD. Another telling fact in the study was that among all youth, those who lived with no primary male in the home (i.e., father or brother) experienced the worst effects of PTSD.

There is a rising tide of crime throughout the nation. Washington DC is not alone. Resurgent drug trafficking, popular culture's violent icons, and the intransigence of entrenched poverty are all contributing factors. There are no easy answers. However, some factors should be considered by churches and community groups to address the rising tide of aggression.

Families need moral valuation. This is the psychosocial dimension of family-oriented ministry. As the Alabama study pointed out, the presence of primary males in households *does* make a difference. Big-brother mentoring programs make a difference. Discussions groups held in Sunday school or other educational environments should encourage freedom of expression in addition to in-depth exploration of biblical morality. Exercises in role playing can teach people to speak kindly and gently, to practice forgiveness, and to avoid situations in which destructive behavior can get out of hand. Ultimately, the church must model that the essential message of Jesus is love, forgiveness, and compassion. Ultimately, the cross says that there are some things worth dying for, but little (if any) worth killing for.

Physical–Medical

Another reality of twenty-first-century America is that African Americans tend to live less healthy lives than do other Americans. Some of the causes of these phenomena are inadequate nutrition, substandard health care, alcohol and drug abuse, and inordinately stressful lives.

The lack of stable, two-parent families exacerbates a number of factors contributing to ill health. Single women with children tend to live at or below the poverty line—which often translates into inadequate prenatal care, increased childhood maladies, and poor nutrition that in turn reduces a child's learning readiness and energy levels in the classroom. As for the health of the parent, any single person, male or female, who must prepare children for day care, transport them on public transportation, and return in the evening after a day's work at some menial job will live a life laced with inordinate stress.

Family instability also leads to such emotional dependencies as alcohol and drug abuse. Alcohol has been the painkiller of choice for poor people since ancient times. Alcohol and drug abuse lead to a greater tendency to less responsible sexual behavior and therefore contribute to soaring pregnancy rates and the proliferation of sexually transmitted disease.

The results of these abuses often lead to two of the principle problems facing black America: prison incarceration and the AIDS epidemic. One reason families are without men is the high percentage of African American males in prison. Unjust laws contribute to that particular phenomenon. Dealing and consuming crack, the drug of choice of poor people, leads to harsher, longer sentences. Recently it has been discovered that long prison tenure is one of the contributing factors to men acquiring bisexual behavior, the so-called down-low phenomenon. At-risk, irresponsible sexual practices along with drug abuse lead to the chief medical problem facing black America, HIV/AIDS. Presently, the fastest rising number of those with HIV/AIDS is African American women.

Another example of the ill health within the black community is the high incidence of smoking-related ailments such as lung cancer, diabetes, and heart disease. Each year 45,000 African Americans die from a preventable smoking related illness.

Consider these alarming statistics:

■ 1.6 million African Americans under the age of 18 will become smokers.

■ 87 percent of lung cancers come from smoking. African American men are 50 percent more likely to develop lung cancer than white men.

■ Smoking elevates cerebrovascular disease, which is highly associated with stroke. Cerebrovascular disease is twice as high among African American men and women as among white men and women.

■ Three out of four black smokers favor menthol cigarettes, and menthol may facilitate the absorption of harmful cigarette smoke constituents.

Don't underestimate the economics of the tobacco industry—and how that industry courts the black community. It isn't only that *Essence, Jet,* and *Ebony* magazines receive proportionally higher profits from cigarette advertisements than comparable "white" magazines. The tobacco industry attempts to maintain a positive image and public support among African Americans by supporting cultural events and making contributions to minority educational institutions, elected officials, civic and community organizations, and scholarship programs.

There are other problems and churches must do more to address them. Silence on the topic of sex is not an option. Sunday school and Christian education classes must make sexuality a primary thrust of learning. Lessons concerning what the Bible instructs about the devastating results of irresponsible sexuality must be integrated throughout church school curricula.

Support for single parents must be another major goal of churches. Affordable day-care centers should be developed, and health ministries that offer immunization programs and testing and screening for such diseases as colorectal cancer, diabetes, high blood pressure, and HIV/AIDS should be implemented.

We may not think of it, but when we read the New Testament,

we find that a major premise of the ministry of Jesus was that everyone is loved by God and that everyone has access to a healthy, stress-free life.

Economics

Then there is the economic area. One hundred and forty years ago, when liberation came to blacks in America, we were promised forty acres and a mule. We are still waiting. There have been some discussions about reparations. Even conservative columnist Charles Krauthammer has raised the flag that this might not be a bad idea. Unfortunately, he sees it as a way to once and for all silence black people about how badly they are treated.

In reality, one of the dragging weights on black families is the continuing economic malaise within the black community. With gas prices at more than three dollars per gallon, health care increasingly out of the reach of the middle class, and decent affordable housing harder and harder to find, families remain beset by economic conditions not of their choosing.

With the rise of the union movement after World War II, many blacks got into the manufacturing sector of the American economy and began to climb the ladder to middle-class life. However, just as manufacturing was improving the economic fortunes of many black families, the captains of American industry anticipated the dwindling of their profits. With the globalization of the economy and such eventualities as NAFTA, cheap foreign labor was brought into the picture. Manufacturing plants relocated to the Far East, Mexico, and China. Many young blacks during the Vietnam era pinned their hopes of middle-class life, as their fathers did, in blue-collar upward mobility in the manufacturing sector—only to discover that for the most part these jobs no longer exist. Following the Vietnam era came the advent of information technology. Computers became king. In addition, under Ronald Reagan, unions lost their power. Unskilled jobs remained largely in the lower end of the service sector (e.g., minimum wage positions at Wendy's and McDonald's).

Rather than cursing the darkness, it is time for our religious communities to fight back. Churches can begin to teach entrepreneurship. When my wife and I went to Kenya a few years ago on a mission trip, the seminar my wife taught was packed with young women who wanted to talk about how to start, manage, and grow businesses. These women in Kenya are clear that working for someone is not the secret; developing one's own cottage industry may not make one rich, but it does give one dignity and freedom.

Our churches can understand that in the history of Judeo-Christian religion, economics has played an important role in the life of the faith. Joseph became second in command to Pharaoh because he had keen business sense. The daughters of Zelophehad were women who insisted on their inheritance from Moses just as male heirs would—and God honored their claim. In the New Testament Lydia was a worker in purple cloth, the most expensive of its time.

As we teach Bible study, values clarification, and communication skills, we need to spend some time instructing families in the sophistications of investing, saving, and developing the business skills to teach our people not to be economic victims but victors. When Jesus was presented at the temple, Mary and Joseph made a sacrifice of two turtle doves, an expensive sacrifice for poor people, but the mother and adoptive father of Jesus understood the need to invest in their children. At Shiloh, we emulate their example, and every time we dedicate a baby, the church takes seven dollars from the offering and starts an account in the credit union for the child. Families are then encouraged to continue to invest in the account. What can your church do to implement the biblical economics of stewardship and investment—in both material and human resources?

In 1985 *The Church in the Life of the Black Family* attempted to address the silence of the black church in the face of rising instances of dysfunctional families. Since that writing, some progress has been made. In the area of government, African Americans have made tremendous strides as black politicians now hold every level of elected and appointed offices. In business, black CEOs have broken through the glass ceiling, even commanding Fortune 500 companies. One could make the case that middle- and upper-income blacks have begun to develop parity with whites. However, AIDs, crime, inadequate education, and rising violence indicate that the church's job is not done. We must continue to preach to get people saved. However, we must also show them, as Moses did with Israel, the pathways that lead out of the earthly wilderness in which we now live.

BIBLIOGRAPHY

CHAPTER 1

Billingsley, Andrew. *Black Families in White America.* Englewood Cliffs, NJ: Prentice-Hall, 1968.

————. *Climbing Jacob's Ladder: The Enduring Legacy of African American Families.* New York: Simon and Schuster, 1992.

Carson, Clayborne. *The Papers of Martin Luther King, Jr. (1956–64),* vol. 1. Berkeley: University of California Press, 1992.

Chatters, Linda M., et al. *Family Life in Black America.* Thousand Oaks, CA: Sage, 1997.

Elshtain, Jean Bethke. *Augustine and the Limits of Politics.* Notre Dame, IN: University of Notre Dame Press, 1995.

Frazier, E. Franklin. *The Free Negro Family.* Nashville: Fisk University Press, 1932.

————. *The Negro Family in Chicago.* Chicago: University of Chicago Press, 1932.

————. *The Negro Family in the United States.* Chicago: University of Chicago Press, 1939.

Gibbs, Jewell T. *Young, Black, and Male in America: An Endangered Species.* Waco, TX: Auburn House, 1988.

Hill, Robert Bernard. *The Strengths of African American Families: Twenty-Five Years Later.* Lanham, MD: University Press of America, 1999.

Logan, Sadye. "Race, Identity, and Black Children: A Developmental Perspective." *Social Casework* 62 (1981): 47–56.

————, ed. *The Black Family: Strengths, Self-Helps, and*

Positive Change. Boulder, CO: Westview Press, Inc., 1996.

Martin, Elmer P., and Martin, Joanne Mitchell. *The Black Extended Family*. Chicago: University of Chicago Press, 1978.

Nobles, W. W. *Africanity and the Black Family*, 2nd ed. Oakland, CA: Institute for the Advanced Study of Black Family Life and Culture, 1985.

Oliver, W. "Black Males and Social Problems." *Journal of Black Studies* 20, no. 1 (September 1989): 15–39.

Roberts, J. Deotis. *Roots of a Black Future: Black Family and Church*. Bowie, MD: J. Deotis Roberts Press, 2002.

Solomon, B. B. *Black Empowerment: Social Work in Oppressed Communities*. New York: Columbia University Press, 1976.

Staples, Robert. *The Black Family: Essays and Studies*. Belmont, CA: Wadsworth, 1970.

Willie, Charles V. *The Family Life of Black People*. Columbus, OH: Merrill, 1970.

CHAPTER 6

Conley, Dalton. *Being Black, Living in the Red: Race, Wealth and Social Policy in America*. Berkeley: University of California Press, 1999.

Jackson, Kenneth T. *The Crabgrass Frontier: The Suburbanization of the United States*. New York: Oxford University Press, 1985.

Levy, Frank, and Richard Michel. *The Economic Future of American Families: Income and Wealth Trends*. Washington, DC: Urban Institute Press, 1991.

Massey, Douglas S., and Nancy A. Denton. *American Apartheid: Segregation and the Making of the Underclass*. Cambridge, MA: Harvard University Press, 1993.

Mellan, Olivia, and Sherry Christie. *Overcoming Overspending: A Winning Plan for Spenders and Their Partners*. New York: Walker and Company, 1997.

Oliver, Melvin L., and Thomas M. Shapiro. *Black*

Wealth/White Wealth: A New Perspective on Racial Inequality.
New York: Routledge, 1995.

Washton, Arnold M., and Donna Boundy. *Willpower Is Not Enough: Understanding and Overcoming Addiction and Compulsion.* New York: HarperCollins, 1990.

CHAPTER 7

Allen-Meares, P., R. Washington and B. Welsh. *Social Work Services in Schools,* 2nd ed. Needham Heights, MA: Allyn & Bacon, 1996.

Anderson, Herbert, and Freda A. Gardner. *Living Alone.* Louisville: Westminster John Knox, 1997.

————. Edward Foley, Bonnie and Robert Schreiter, Miller-McLemore eds. *Mutuality Matters: Family, Faith, and Just Love.* Lanham, MD: Rowman and Littlefield, 2003.

Billingsley, Andrew. *Climbing Jacob's Ladder.* New York: Simon & Schuster, 1992.

————. *Mighty Like a River: The Black Church and Social Reform.* New York: Oxford University Press, 1999.

Broman, C. L. "Race Differences in Professional Help Seeking." *American Journal of Community Psychology* 14, no. 4 (1987): 473–89.

Bultmann, Rudolf. *Jesus and the Word.* New York: Scribner's Sons, 1958.

Carter, Les, and Frank Minirth. *The Anger Workbook for Christian Parents.* San Francisco: Jossey-Bass, 2004.

Chadiha, L. "Black Husbands' Economic Problems and Resiliency during the Transition to Marriage." *Families in Society* 73 (1992): 542–52.

Constantino, G., R. G. Malgady, and L. H. Rogler. "Culturally Sensitive Psychotherapy for Puerto Rican Children and Adolescents: A Program of Treatment Outcome Research." *Journal of Consulting and Clinical Psychology* 58, no. 6 (1990): 704–12.

Davis, J. E., and W. J. Jordan "The Effects of School Context,

Structure, and Experiences on African American Males in Middle and High School." *Journal of Negro Education* 63 (1994): 570–87.

Davis, L. *Black and Single*. Chicago: Noble, 1993.

Davis, Larry E., ed. *Working with African American Males: A Guide to Practice*. Thousand Oaks, CA: Sage, 1999.

Delpit, L. D. "The Silenced Dialogue: Power and Pedagogy in Educating Other People's Children." *Harvard Educational Review* 58 (1988): 280–98.

Douglas, Kelly Brown. *Sexuality and the Black Church: A Womanist Perspective*. Maryknoll, NY: Orbis, 2002.

Edelman, M. W. *Families in Peril*. Cambridge, MA: Harvard University Press, 1987.

Faller, K. C. *Child Sexual Abuse: An Interdisciplinary Manual for Diagnosis, Case Management, and Treatment*. New York: Columbia University Press, 1988.

Feagin, J. R., and M. P. Sikes. *Living with Racism: The Black Middle-Class Experience*. Boston: Beacon, 1994.

Fordham, S., and J. Ogbu. "Black Students' School Success: Coping with the Burden of 'Acting White.'" *Urban Review* 18 (1986): 176–206.

Friedman, Edwin H. *Generation to Generation: Family Process in Church and Synagogue*. New York: Guilford, 1985.

Gibbs, Jewell T., ed. *Young, Black, and Male in America: An Endangered Species*. Waco, TX: Auburn House, 1988.

Gil, E., and T. C. Johnson. *Sexualized Children*. Rockville, MD: Launch, 1993.

Godsey, John D. *The Theology of Dietrich Bonhoeffer*. Philadelphia: Westminster, 1960.

Hacker, A. *Two Nations: Black and White, Separate, Hostile, Unequal*. New York: Scribner, 1992.

Hauk, Gary H. *Family Enrichment in Your Church*. Nashville: Convention, 1988.

Hewlett, Sylvia Ann, and Cornell West. *The War against Parents*. New York: Mariner, 1998.

Hill, Paul, Jr. *Coming of Age: African American Male Rites-of-Passage*. Chicago: African American Images, 1992.

Hilliard, A. G. "A Framework for Focused Counseling on the African American Man." *Journal of Non-White Concerns in Personnel and Guidance* 13 (1985): 72–78.

Hutchinson, Earl O. *The Assassination of the Black Male Image*. New York: Simon and Schuster, 1994.

June, Lee N., ed. *The Black Family—Past, Present, and Future*. Grand Rapids: Zondervan, 1991.

Kelcourse, Felicity, ed. *Human Development and Faith: Life-Cycle Stages of Body, Mind, and Soul*. St. Louis, MO: Chalice, 2004.

Kunjufu, Jawanza. *Countering the Conspiracy to Destroy Black Boys*, 2 vols. Chicago: African American Images, 1986, 1988.

Leake, D. O., and B. L. Leake. "Islands of Hope: Milwaukee's African-American Immersion Schools." *Journal of Negro Education* 61 (1992): 24–29.

LeCompte, M., and S. Goebel. "Can Bad Data Produce Good Program Planning? An Analysis of Record Keeping on School Dropouts." *Education and Urban Society* 19 (1987): 250–68.

Livingston, David J. *Healing Violent Men: A Model for Christian Communities*. Minneapolis: Fortress, 2002.

Mandell, J. G., and L. Damon. *Group Treatment for Sexually Abused Children*. New York: Guilford, 1989.

Massey, D., and N. Denton. *American Apartheid*. Cambridge, MA: Harvard University Press, 1993.

McDavis, Roderick J., Woodrow M. Parker and W. J. Parker. "Counseling African Americans." In *Experiencing and Counseling Multicultural and Diverse Populations*, ed. Nicholas Vace. Muncie, IN: Accelerated Development, 1994.

Mincy, Ronald B. *Nurturing Young Black Males: Challenges to Agencies, Programs, and Social Policy*. Washington, DC: Urban Institute Press, 1994.

National Research Council. *A Common Destiny: Blacks and*

American Society. Washington, DC: National Academy Press, 1989.

Neighbors, H. W. "Seeking Professional Help for Personal Problems: Black Americans' Use of Health and Mental Health Services." *Community Mental Health Journal* 2, no. 3 (1985): 156–66.

Newman, Susan. *Oh God! A Black Woman's Guide to Sex and Spirituality.* New York: One World/Ballantine Books, 2002.

Noguera, P. "Reducing and Preventing Youth Violence: An Analysis of Causes and an Assessment of Successful Programs." *Wellness Lectures.* Oakland: University of California Press, 1995.

Oyserman, D., L. Gant, and J. Ager. "A Socially Contextualized Model of African American Identity: Possible Selves and School Persistence." *Journal of Personality & Social Psychology* 69 (1995): 1216–32.

Patterson, Sheron C. *Put On Your Crown: A Black Woman's Guide to Living Single.* Cleveland: Pilgrim, 2006.

Perkins, James C. *Building Up Zion's Walls: Ministry for Empowering the African American Family.* Edited by Jean Alicia Elster. Valley Forge, PA: Judson, 1999.

Porter, E. *Treating the Young Male Victims of Sexual Assault: Issues and Intervention Strategies.* Syracuse, NY: Safer Society, 1986.

Porter, Frances S., Linda C. Black, and Suzanne M. Sgroi. "Treatment of the Sexually Abused Child." In *Handbook of Clinical Intervention in Child Sexual Abuse,* ed. Suzanne M. Sgroi. Lexington, MA: Lexington, 1982.

Roberts, J. Deotis. *Africentric Christianity.* Valley Forge, PA: Judson, 2000.

———. *A Black Political Theology.* Philadelphia: Westminster, 1974.

———. *Black Theology in Dialogue.* Philadelphia: Westminster, 1987.

———. *Prophethood of Black Believers: An African American Political Theology for Ministry.* Louisville: Westminster John Knox, 1994.

Richardson, Ronald W. *Creating a Healthier Church—Family Systems Theory, Leadership, and Congregational Life.* Minneapolis: Fortress, 1996.

Rivera, D., J. Jackson, and J. Jackson. "Our Current Concerns." *National Rainbow Coalition Newsletter* 12 (1993): 1.

Rogers, C. M., and T. Terry. "Clinical Interventions with Boy Victims of Sexual Abuse." In *Victims of Sexual Aggression*, ed. Irving R. Stuart. New York: Van Nostrand Reinhold, 1984.

Roper, W. "The Prevention of Minority Youth Violence Must Begin Despite Risks and Imperfect Understanding." *Public Health Reports* 106, no. 3 (May–June 1991): 229–31.

Rubin, R., Andrew Billingsley, and Cleopatra Howard Caldwell. "The Role of the Black Church in Working with Black Adolescents." *Adolescence* 29, no. 114 (Summer 1994): 251.

Schinke, S. P., G. J. Botvin, and M. A. Orlandi. *Substance Abuse in Children and Adolescents: Evaluation and Intervention.* Newbury Park, CA: Sage Publishers, 1991.

Sebold, J. "Indicators of Child Sexual Abuse in Males: Social Casework." *Journal of Contemporary Social Work* 68 (1987): 75–80.

Slavin, R. E., N. A. Madden, L. J. Dolan, B. A. Wasch, S. M. Ross, and L. J. Smith. "Whenever and Wherever We Choose: The Replication of Success for All." *Phi Delta Kappan* 75 (April 1994): 639–47.

Smith, Wallace Charles. *The Church in the Life of the Black Family.* Valley Forge, PA: Judson, 1985.

Spivak, H., D. Prothrow-Stith, and A. Hausman. "Dying Is No Accident." *Pediatric Clinics of North America* 35, no. 6 (December 1988): 1339–47.

Stone, Howard W., ed. *Strategies for Brief Pastoral Counseling.* Minneapolis: Fortress, 2001.

Sturkie, K. "Structured Group Treatment for Sexually Abused Children." *Health and Social Work* 8 (1983): 299–308.

Szapocznik, J., and W. Kurtines. "Acculturation, Biculturalism, and Adjustment among Cuban Americans." In *Acculturation: Theory, Models, and Some New Findings,* ed. A. M. Padilla.

Taylor, Robert Joseph, James S. Jackson, and Linda M. Chatters. *Family Life in Black America.* Newbury Park, CA: Sage, 1997.

Thurman, Howard. *Jesus and the Disinherited.* Richmond, IN: Friends United, 1981. First published by Abingdon Press, 1949.

Tobias, R. "Educating Black Urban Adolescents." In *Black Adolescents,* ed. R. Jones. Berkeley, CA: Cobb & Henry, 1989.

Turner, S., E. Norman, and S. Zunz. (1995). "Enhancing Resiliency in Girls and Boys: A Case for Gender Specific Adolescent Prevention Programming." *Journal of Primary Prevention* 16, no. 8 (1995): 25–38.

Walker, Clarence. *Breaking Strongholds in the African American Family: Strategies for Spiritual Warfare.* Grand Rapids: Zondervan, 1996.

Walker, Elizabeth. "Pastoral Counseling with Some African American Women." Unpublished dissertation. Atlanta: Interdenominational Theological Center, 2000.

Washington, James M., ed. *The Essential Writings and Speeches of Martin Luther King, Jr.* New York: HarperCollins, 1986.

Weaver, Andrew J., Linda A. Revilla, and Harold G. Koenig *Counseling Families Across the Stages of Life: A Handbook for Pastors and Other Helping Professionals.* Nashville: Abingdon, 2002.

West, Cornel. *Race Matters.* New York: Vintage, 1993.

Whetstone, M. "What Happens When the Woman Makes More than the Man?" *Ebony* (1996): 30–34.

Wigger, J. Bradley. *The Power of God at Home: Nurturing Children in Love and Grace.* San Francisco: Jossey-Bass, 2003.

————. *Together We Pray: A Prayer Book For Families*. St. Louis, MO: Chalice, 2005.

Wilmore, Gayraud, ed. *Black Men in Prison: The Response of the African American Church*. Atlanta: ITC Press, 1990.

Wilson, A. *Understanding Black Adolescent Male Violence*. New York: Afrikan World Infosystems, 1992.

Wilson, Julius W. *When Work Disappears*. New York: Alfred Knopf, 1996.

Wimberly, Anne Streaty, ed. *Keeping It Real: Working with Today's Black Youth*. Nashville: Abingdon, 2005.

Wimberly, Edward P. *Honoring African American Elders: A Ministry in the Soul Community*. San Francisco: Jossey-Bass, 1997.

————. *Pastoral Counseling and Spiritual Values: A Black Point of View*. Nashville: Abingdon, 1982.

————. *Relational Refugees: Alienation and Reincorporation in African American Churches and Communities*. Nashville: Abingdon, 2000.

ABOUT THE CONTRIBUTORS

Lorraine Blackman, PhD, associate professor at the University of Indiana School of Social Work, is a much-sought-after speaker and presenter at conferences across the nation. She specializes in marriage enrichment and overall family health.

Michael L. Cook, MDiv, founder and CEO of Alexander-Mackenzie, LLC, is a graduate of Duke University Divinity School. Cook established Alexander-Mackenzie as a consulting organization specializing in providing the general public with independent and objective consumer advice on financial matters.

Johnny B. Hill, PhD, assistant professor of theology at Louisville Presbyterian Theological Seminary, in Louisville, Kentucky, is an ordained Baptist minister who also serves on the Justice and Advocacy Commission of the National Council of Churches, USA.

Sherrill McMillan, MD, serves as director of counseling at the Metropolitan Baptist Church in Washington DC. She also coordinates The Garment's Hem, Inc., in Prince George's County, Maryland, a program that seeks to revive and rehabilitate individuals and families struggling with emotional, psychological, and mental challenges.

Wallace Charles Smith, DMin, president of Palmer Theological Seminary and pastor of the historic Shiloh Baptist Church in downtown Washington DC, is a sought-after preacher, speaker, and lecturer. Dr. Smith has been an outspoken proponent of the church and black family life for several decades.

Elizabeth Johnson Walker, PhD, associate professor of pastoral care and counseling at Louisville Presbyterian Theological Seminary, is a practicing marriage and family therapist. Walker is an expert in pastoral care and in marriage and family therapy.

Rueben Warren, DDS, is associate director at the Institute for Faith-Health Leadership at the Interdenominational Theological Center in Atlanta.

Anne Streaty Wimberly, PhD, currently serves as professor of church history at the Interdenominational Theological Center in Atlanta. She has published widely in her field, including work on the church and hip-hop culture. Her interests include youth culture, family life, and social justice issues.

Edward P. Wimberly, PhD, vice provost, academic dean, and professor of pastoral care and counseling at the Interdenominational Theological Center, has written extensively about counseling, pastoral care, family life, and youth.